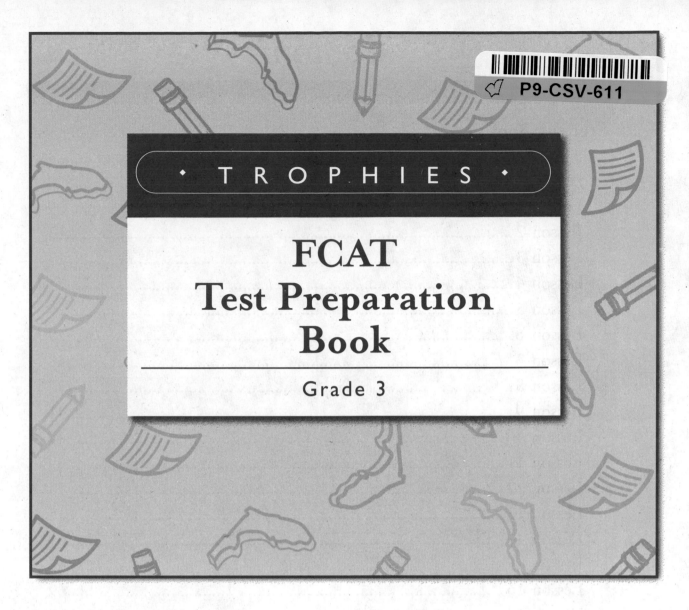

· T R O P H I E S ·

FCAT
Test Preparation
Book

Grade 3

Printed in the United States of America

ISBN 0-15-326274-5

12 13 14 15 16 085 10 09 08 07 06

Orlando   Boston   Dallas   Chicago   San Diego

Visit *The Learning Site!*
www.harcourtschool.com

© Harcourt

Contents

Student Book

© Harcourt

Support for Writing

Use the scoring chart below to evaluate your writing. The scoring is based on a six-point scale. A score of six is the highest score, and a score of one is the lowest score. The scores are based on four categories:

- Focus
- Organization
- Support
- Conventions

Your writing needs to match a score's description to receive that score.

FCAT SCORING RUBRIC

	Focus	Organization	Support	Conventions
6	All the ideas in my writing tell about the same thing.	All the ideas in my writing are in a logical order.	My writing has many colorful words and specific details.	My writing has many kinds of sentences. I use correct capitalization, punctuation, and spelling.
5	Most of the ideas in my writing tell about the same thing.	Most of the ideas in my writing are in a logical order.	My writing has enough colorful words and specific details.	My writing has a few kinds of sentences. I mostly use correct capitalization, punctuation, and spelling.
4	Many of the ideas in my writing tell about the same thing.	Many of the ideas in my writing are in a logical order.	My writing has some colorful words and some specific details.	My writing has one or two kinds of sentences. I sometimes use correct capitalization, punctuation, and spelling.
3	Some of the ideas in my writing tell about the same thing.	Some of the ideas in my writing are in a logical order.	My writing has a few colorful words and details that could be more specific.	My writing has mostly just one kind of sentence. I sometimes use correct capitalization, punctuation, and spelling.
2	Many of the ideas in my writing are not about the same thing.	Many of the ideas in my writing are not in a logical order.	My writing has very few colorful words and details that are not specific.	My writing has mostly just one kind of sentence. I rarely use correct capitalization, punctuation, and spelling.
1	Most of the ideas in my writing are not about the same thing.	Most of the ideas in my writing are not in a logical order.	My writing does not have colorful words and specific details.	My writing has just one kind of sentence. I do not use correct capitalization, punctuation, and spelling.

Use the charts below to evaluate your responses to open-ended test questions. Each chart is based on a point scale. The descriptions explain requirements for each score point.

Rubric for Short-Answer Questions

READ
THINK
EXPLAIN

2 Points

My response shows that I understand the ideas presented. My response is correct and complete.

1 Point

My response shows that I understand some of the ideas presented. My response is correct, but it is not complete.

0 Points

I have not given a response, my response is not correct, or my response does not make sense.

Rubric for Extended-Response Questions

READ
THINK
EXPLAIN

4 Points

My response shows that I understand the ideas presented. My response is correct and complete.

3 Points

My response shows that I understand the ideas presented. My response is correct, but I do not give enough details.

2 Points

My response shows that I understand some of the ideas presented. My response is correct, but it is not complete.

1 Point

My response shows that I understand a few of the ideas presented. My response is not complete and has many mistakes.

0 Points

I have not given a response, my response is not correct, or my response does not make sense.

Dear Student,

Once a year, the students in your school take a special test. This test helps teachers and the principal know what you are learning.

Taking the test is easier when you know how. This book will help you learn how to take the tests. It will give you practice in listening carefully, reading carefully, and following directions.

Take some hints from the tortoise and the hare. The tortoise reads carefully and chooses the best answers. The hare is careless and makes mistakes. Will you be like the tortoise or the hare?

✔ LISTEN carefully.

✔ READ carefully.

✔ CHOOSE the best answer.

✔ MARK answer choices carefully.

✔ CHECK your work.

Getting Prepared

The tortoise is always prepared and ready to pay attention to the teacher. Think about how you can be ready for a test. Then read the tortoise's tips below.

Tips for Listening

1. Sit quietly.

2. Look at the speaker.

3. Listen for directions.

4. Ignore other students.

5. Listen to important information.

Tips for Taking a Test

1. Sit up straight and comfortably in your chair.

2. Keep your eyes on the teacher or on the test booklet.

3. Have your sharpened pencils ready.

Important Words

You will see some important words when you take tests. These words tell you what to do. Look at the words and pictures. Then answer the questions. Remember to mark each answer choice as the tortoise would.

1 What word or words tell you to keep working?

- ○ GO ON
- ○ DIRECTIONS
- ○ STOP
- ○ SAMPLE

2 What word or words tell you to put your pencil down?

- ○ GO ON
- ○ DIRECTIONS
- ○ STOP
- ○ SAMPLE

© Harcourt

Fill in the checklist to show what you will do when you take a test.

I will

- ☐ listen carefully.
- ☐ read carefully.
- ☐ follow directions.
- ☐ mark answers carefully.
- ☐ begin where told.
- ☐ begin when told.
- ☐ stop when told.
- ☐ guess carefully.
- ☐ check my answers.
- ☐ pay attention only to the teacher and the test.
- ☐ do the best I can.

_____

Name

**Read the story about "The Best of Friends."
Then answer Numbers 1 through 8.**

The Best of Friends

No one thinks it's strange now. But at first, people would stop to stare at the little bird riding on the back of the big dog. About a year ago, Brian's dog, Rudy, saw the little bird fall out of a tree. Ever since then, Rudy and his bird friend, Judy, have been together.

When a neighbor's cat scared Judy out of the tree, the bird fell to the ground. Rudy barked and chased the cat away but soon ran into Coco, a bulldog that lived in the house next door.

Coco heard the noise that Rudy and the cat made and wanted to join the fun. He chased Rudy back to the yard. Rudy was afraid Coco would find the bird on the ground, but by that time Brian had found the two dogs and told Coco to go home.

Rudy whined and cried when he went up to the bird. "What's wrong, Rudy?" Brian asked.

Rudy pushed aside the grass around the bird with his nose.

"What have we got here?" Brian asked as he looked closer. He could tell that one of the bird's wings was hurt.

Rudy barked as Brian took the bird away.

TEST-TAKING TIP
To understand the story, ask questions as you read. Why would people think it is strange for a bird and a dog to be friends?

TEST-TAKING TIP
When you read stories that have dialogue, pay attention to who is talking. Stories with many characters may become confusing.

Go On

"Don't worry, Rudy. I'm just taking him to Uncle Ken," Brian told him. Uncle Ken was a <u>veterinarian</u>. Brian always took hurt animals to his uncle for help. Brian hoped that one day he would be an animal doctor like his uncle.

Uncle Ken wrapped the wing. He told Brian how to care for the bird until she could fly again. Brian borrowed a cage and put the bird in his room.

After two weeks, Judy was better. It wasn't long before she was flying around the yard. When Judy was tired, she would rest on Rudy's back. Before long Rudy and Judy were good friends.

Now answer Numbers 1 through 8. Base your answers on the story "The Best of Friends."

1 Most of this story takes place in or near ◄

   Ⓐ Rudy's yard.

   Ⓑ Uncle Ken's house.

   Ⓒ Coco's yard.

   Ⓓ a bush.

2 Brian is best described as ◄

   Ⓕ mean.

   Ⓖ caring.

   Ⓗ afraid.

   Ⓘ worried.

TEST-TAKING TIP
Many things happened in the story. You may have forgotten where they all took place. Look back at the beginning of the story to find out.

TEST-TAKING TIP
Read the answer choices. Which word describes how Brian treats Judy and Rudy?

© Harcourt

Go On

Grade 3

Name _____

3 What causes Coco to chase Rudy?

Ⓐ He sees the bird in its nest.

Ⓑ He wants to see what is happening.

Ⓒ He chases Brian and finds Rudy.

Ⓓ A cat chases Coco.

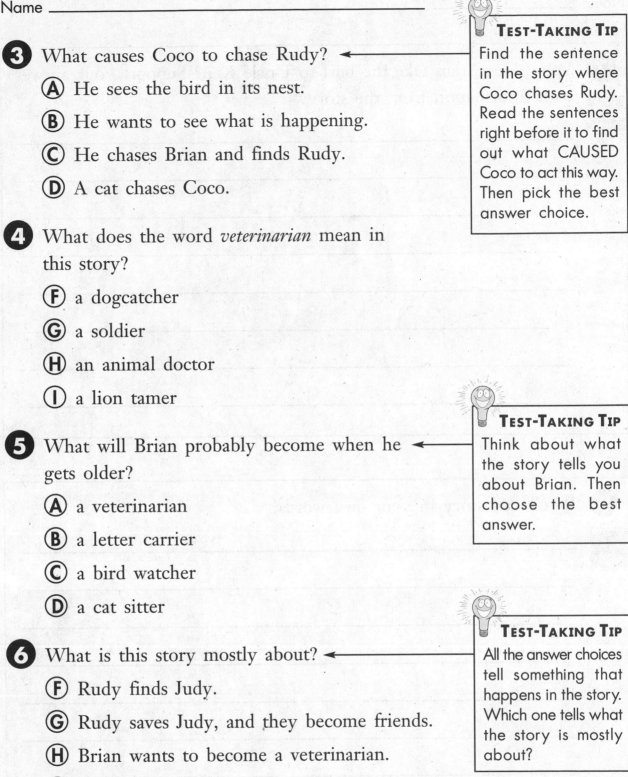

TEST-TAKING TIP

Find the sentence in the story where Coco chases Rudy. Read the sentences right before it to find out what CAUSED Coco to act this way. Then pick the best answer choice.

4 What does the word *veterinarian* mean in this story?

Ⓕ a dogcatcher

Ⓖ a soldier

Ⓗ an animal doctor

Ⓘ a lion tamer

5 What will Brian probably become when he gets older?

Ⓐ a veterinarian

Ⓑ a letter carrier

Ⓒ a bird watcher

Ⓓ a cat sitter

TEST-TAKING TIP

Think about what the story tells you about Brian. Then choose the best answer.

6 What is this story mostly about?

Ⓕ Rudy finds Judy.

Ⓖ Rudy saves Judy, and they become friends.

Ⓗ Brian wants to become a veterinarian.

Ⓘ Coco wants to play.

TEST-TAKING TIP

All the answer choices tell something that happens in the story. Which one tells what the story is mostly about?

© Harcourt

Go On

Lesson 1

7 Why does Brian take the bird to Uncle Ken? Support your answer with information from the story.

READ
THINK
EXPLAIN

_____

_____

_____

_____

_____

_____

_____

8 Retell this story in your own words.

READ
THINK
EXPLAIN

_____

_____

_____

_____

_____

_____

_____

STOP

Grade 3

Read the article "Paper Eagles." Then answer Numbers 1 through 5.

Paper Eagles

Kites were first made by a carpenter who lived in China almost three thousand years ago. His name was Gong Shuban. It is said that he made a wooden kite strong enough to carry a person in the air. This kite was used to find out where the enemy might be during a war. The first kite was called a "wooden eagle." Today, the Chinese word for kite means "paper eagle."

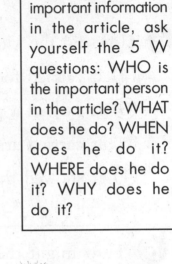

TEST-TAKING TIP
To remember the important information in the article, ask yourself the 5 W questions: WHO is the important person in the article? WHAT does he do? WHEN does he do it? WHERE does he do it? WHY does he do it?

1 Why did the author write "Paper Eagles"?

Ⓐ to convince people to build kites

Ⓑ to get people to join a kite club

Ⓒ to tell a sad story about wartime

Ⓓ to tell the history of kites

TEST-TAKING TIP
The article doesn't say why the kite was called a wooden eagle. Use what you know about eagles and kites to decide why people gave the kite that name.

2 Why did people call the first kite a *wooden eagle*?

Ⓕ It could fly.

Ⓖ It helped Gong Shuban hunt.

Ⓗ It had feathers.

Ⓘ It was very large.

Go On

3 The name "paper eagle" makes kites seem ←

Ⓐ alive.

Ⓑ shy.

Ⓒ colorful.

Ⓓ fat.

4 How did the kite help in wartime? ←

Ⓕ It carried food to prisoners in towers.

Ⓖ It carried a person in the air.

Ⓗ It carried armies to battle.

Ⓘ It showed the direction of the wind.

5 How might the "wooden eagle" have helped a passenger spot enemies in the distance?

READ
THINK
EXPLAIN

_____

_____

_____

_____

_____

_____

_____

_____

Go On

Grade 3

Read the poem "A Wish." Then answer Numbers 6 through 10.

A Wish

Saturday I flew my kite
on a hilltop high.
It leaped up like a dancer
and sailed across the sky.

When it dips and bobs along,
flying looks so easy!
I wish that I could soar like that
when the day is breezy.

6 Which of the following features shows you ← that this is a poem?

Ⓐ It is long.

Ⓑ It rhymes.

Ⓒ It tells a story.

Ⓓ It has a title.

7 What does the TITLE tell you about the poem? ←

Ⓕ The kite is really a person.

Ⓖ The writer of the poem hopes for something.

Ⓗ Dancers and kites are a lot alike.

Ⓘ Hilltops are good places to fly kites.

TEST-TAKING TIP
Some of the answer choices are true about stories as well as poems. Read through all the answer choices. Then pick the answer that is true for poems only.

TEST-TAKING TIP
To answer this question correctly, read the title again. Remember that the title of a poem often tells its main idea. Decide what it helps you know about the poem. Then read through the answer choices and pick the correct answer.

© Harcourt

Go On

8 The kite is like a dancer because it ◄────

Ⓐ moves gracefully.

Ⓑ has a tail.

Ⓒ smiles widely.

Ⓓ sails on a breezy day.

9 What does the writer want to do when he sees the kite in the air?

Ⓕ sing

Ⓖ dance

Ⓗ fly

Ⓘ sleep

10 Do the rhymes make the poem easier to read? Explain your answer.

READ
THINK
EXPLAIN

_____

_____

_____

_____

_____

_____

_____

_____

© Harcourt

STOP

Grade 3

Read the article "Something in
the Air." Then answer
Numbers 1 through 7.

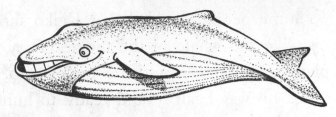

Something in the Air

Keiko knew something was going on. The people
who took care of him were planning something.
Every day new people came and took measurements.
They checked Keiko's teeth, skin, and dorsal fin over
and over again.

When he was young and in the wild, Keiko's fin ←
had been tall, straight, and proud. He was just like
the other orca whales in his pod. However, Keiko
had been caught before he was fully grown. People
wanted to teach him to do tricks for visitors. He
lived in a small pool for many years. Over time,
his fin had drooped far over to one side, and now
it was bent that way for good.

Keiko was unhappy in his small pool. Then one ←
day, a film company came to the pool. They filmed
Keiko doing some of his tricks, and sometimes they
filmed a young boy doing what looked like other
tricks. Then they left, and Keiko went back to
his routine.

What Keiko didn't know was that they had been
filming a movie called *Free Willy*. The movie was
about a whale who <u>escapes</u> from his pool and returns
to the wild. After the movie came out, people learned
about Keiko and his small pool. News stories said
that he was ill and bored.

> **TEST-TAKING TIP**
> Don't try to remember
> every detail and
> event in the article.
> Read it once to get
> the main idea. Then
> as you answer the
> questions, look back
> at the article as often
> as you need to.

> **TEST-TAKING TIP**
> The words *then
> one day* usually tell
> you that something
> different is about to
> happen. Watch for
> more signal words
> in the article.

© Harcourt

Go On

Some people decided that Keiko should be freed, just like the whale in the movie. They decided on a plan. First, they would move Keiko to a larger pool. Once he was healthy and ready to hunt for his own food, he would move again. This time Keiko would go all the way to Iceland, near the place where he was captured. He would have a huge pool located in the ocean. When he was ready, Keiko would finally be set free into the wild.

Soon, his whole world would change, and he would be happy again.

Now answer Numbers 1 through 7. Base your answers on the article "Something in the Air."

1 This article is mostly about ◄——

 Ⓐ an orca whale.

 Ⓑ the Pacific Ocean.

 Ⓒ how to make a movie.

 Ⓓ ocean plants.

2 Before he was caught, Keiko ◄——

 Ⓕ did tricks for the crowd.

 Ⓖ made a movie.

 Ⓗ swam with other whales.

 Ⓘ got sick.

TEST-TAKING TIP
Some of these things do not appear in the article. Cross them out first. Then choose your answer.

TEST-TAKING TIP
The article tells events in order, from first to last. To find out what Keiko did BEFORE he was caught, look near the beginning of the article.

© Harcourt

Go On

Grade 3

3 How does Keiko feel in his small pool?

   Ⓐ hungry

   Ⓑ happy

   Ⓒ tired

   Ⓓ sad

4 In this article, *escapes* means ◄——

   Ⓕ gets away.

   Ⓖ makes noises.

   Ⓗ eats.

   Ⓘ sleeps.

TEST-TAKING TIP

Don't worry if you don't know the meaning of a word. Read the whole sentence to look for clues. The words *from his pool* and *returns to the wild* give you a hint about what *escapes* means.

5 When he leaves his tiny pool, Keiko will probably

   Ⓐ feel better.

   Ⓑ swim faster.

   Ⓒ grow.

   Ⓓ do tricks.

6 As part of the plan to return Keiko to the wild, ◄—— where will Keiko move first?

   Ⓕ the ocean

   Ⓖ a zoo

   Ⓗ a larger pool

   Ⓘ a pool in the ocean

TEST-TAKING TIP

Keiko will be moved to two new homes before he returns to the wild. Both places appear here. Be sure to pick the place he will be moved to FIRST.

Go On

© Harcourt

7 **READ THINK EXPLAIN** Lots of people know about Keiko since he starred in *Free Willy*. Do you think more attention will be paid to the care of whales in pools? Support your answer with information from the article.

_____

_____

_____

_____

_____

_____

_____

_____

_____

_____

_____

STOP

Grade 3

Name _____

**Read the article "Babe Didrikson Zaharias."
Then answer Numbers 1 through 5.**

Babe Didrikson Zaharias

Some people say that Babe Didrikson Zaharias was the best athlete of all time. She was a great runner, jumper, diver, bowler, and roller skater. Babe beat most people at baseball, basketball, and golf, too!

Her real name was Mildred. People started calling her Babe when she was 12. At that time, she was playing baseball and hitting many long home runs. She reminded people of Babe Ruth, the great baseball player.

Then she went to the Olympics. She won medals for the high jump, the hurdles, and the javelin throw. She won two first-place medals and one second-place medal.

Babe got many prizes for her skills. Sports reporters even named her the top woman athlete in a hundred years!

TEST-TAKING TIP
Babe played a lot of sports. Don't try to remember them all. You can always look back at the story if you need to know them.

1 What is this article mostly about?

Ⓐ the Olympics

Ⓑ baseball stars

Ⓒ playing basketball

Ⓓ a woman sports star

2 People called Mildred "Babe" because

Ⓕ she was very young.

Ⓖ she played baseball.

Ⓗ she reminded them of Babe Ruth.

Ⓘ she won Olympic medals.

TEST-TAKING TIP
Be sure to think about all the answer choices. *G* might seem correct at first, but another answer is better.

Go On

© Harcourt

3 How many medals did Babe win at the Olympics?

    Ⓐ one   Ⓒ three

    Ⓑ two   Ⓓ four

TEST-TAKING TIP
Read the question carefully. Babe won different kinds of medals. How many medals did she win in all?

4 Imagine that your teacher asked you to write a report about Babe. What would be most helpful to you?

    Ⓕ a map that shows where the Winter Olympics have been held

    Ⓖ a chart that shows where and when Babe won her medals

    Ⓗ a photograph of the Olympic flag

    Ⓘ a diagram that shows how to place players in a baseball field

TEST-TAKING TIP
Study each answer choice. Which one would give the most information about Babe Didrikson?

5 Why do you think the author wrote this article about Babe?

READ
THINK
EXPLAIN

_____

_____

_____

_____

_____

_____

_____

Go On

Grade 3

© Harcourt

Name _____

Read the poem "A Girl Called Babe."
Then answer Numbers 6 through 10.

A Girl Called Babe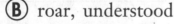

TEST-TAKING TIP
Be sure to read the title. Otherwise, you won't know who the writer is talking about in the first sentence.

She stepped up to the plate
and gave a mighty swing.
Then WHACK!
The ball sailed over the fence,
and her team began to sing!

The crowd let out a roar.
Now they understood
why people called her Babe.
She really was that good!

TEST-TAKING TIP
Read each pair of words softly to yourself. Which ones sound the most alike?

6 Which words from the poem rhyme, or sound alike?

Ⓐ plate, fence

Ⓑ roar, understood

Ⓒ Babe, good

Ⓓ swing, sing

7 What happened right AFTER the ball sailed over the fence?

Ⓕ Babe swung the bat.

Ⓖ Babe stepped up to the plate.

Ⓗ Babe's team began to sing.

Ⓘ The crowd roared loudly.

Go On

8 What makes the crowd roar?

(A) Babe steps up to the plate.

(B) Babe hits a home run.

(C) The crowd does not like the other team.

(D) The crowd is getting bored and restless.

9 In the poem, which word makes the sound of a bat hitting a ball?

(F) plate

(G) WHACK

(H) sing

(I) understood

TEST-TAKING TIP

Read the answer choices softly to yourself. Listen to the sounds they make. Which one sounds most like a bat hitting a ball?

10

READ
THINK
EXPLAIN

You just read an article about Babe and a poem about Babe. How are they ALIKE? How are they DIFFERENT? Explain your answer.

_____

_____

_____

_____

_____

_____

_____

_____

STOP

© Harcourt

Grade 3

Read the story "Making Popcorn Together" and the directions. Then answer Numbers 1 through 8.

Making Popcorn Together

Elena and Josh wanted to watch a movie and eat a snack.

They looked on the shelves in the kitchen and found a package of microwave popcorn. Elena read the directions out loud.

First, Josh and Elena removed the plastic <u>overwrap</u>. They unfolded the bag and placed it in the center of the microwave oven.

Then, they started the microwave. They listened carefully for the popping sounds. When the popping slowed down, they turned off the microwave and removed the bag. They kept their hands away from the steam as they opened the bag.

They poured the popcorn into a large bowl. Then they went to watch a movie.

TEST-TAKING TIP
There are two ways to decide what *overwrap* is. You can use what you know about word parts. You can also read the sentence again and decide what the word *overwrap* probably means.

TEST-TAKING TIP
Underline words like *first* and *then*. They will help you find the steps in the story.

TEST-TAKING TIP
This list of directions has bullets, or black dots. They make the steps easier to read.

DIRECTIONS

- Remove the plastic <u>overwrap</u>.
- Unfold the bag. Place it in the center of the microwave oven.
- Set the microwave oven to high. Popping time is from 2 to 5 minutes, depending on the oven. Listen carefully. Stop the oven when popping slows to 1 or 2 seconds between pops.
- Remove the bag from the microwave. BE CAREFUL! IT'S VERY HOT! Open the bag by pulling opposite corners. Keep your hands and face away from the hot steam that will escape.

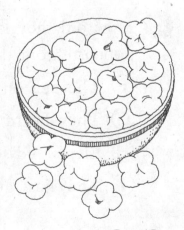

Go On

Name _____

Now answer Numbers 1 through 8. Base your answers on the story "Making Popcorn Together."

1 The story is mostly about

TEST-TAKING TIP
All the answers talk about popcorn. Which answer talks about popcorn the same way the story does?

   Ⓐ flavored popcorn.

   Ⓑ popcorn necklaces.

   Ⓒ eating popcorn.

   Ⓓ making popcorn.

2 In the story and in the directions, an *overwrap* is

   Ⓕ a warm coat to wear outside.

   Ⓖ a box made of paper.

   Ⓗ something that goes over another wrapping.

   Ⓘ gift wrap.

3 At the beginning of the story, what did Josh and Elena want to do?

TEST-TAKING TIP
The words AT THE BEGINNING OF THE STORY are important. Skim the first few sentences of the story to find the answer to this question.

   Ⓐ play a game and watch TV

   Ⓑ watch a movie and eat a snack

   Ⓒ do their homework

   Ⓓ make dinner

4 How did they know it was time to remove the popcorn from the microwave oven?

   Ⓕ The bell on the microwave rang.

   Ⓖ They heard the popping slow down.

   Ⓗ Elena told Josh it was time.

   Ⓘ They just guessed what time it was.

Go On

© Harcourt

Name _____

5 Which word describes Josh and Elena's actions in the kitchen?

    (A) careless   (C) uncaring

    (B) careful   (D) caring

TEST-TAKING TIP
Read the answer choices. Then think about how Josh and Elena act in the kitchen. Choose the best answer to the question.

6 To open the bag, you need to

    (F) pull the opposite corners.

    (G) cut it with a pair of scissors.

    (H) place it back in the microwave.

    (I) remove the plastic overwrap.

TEST-TAKING TIP
To answer this question, you need to decide where to look for the answer. Since the question is not about Josh or Elena, you should look at the directions.

7 Under which word would you look in an encyclopedia to find out about the history of popcorn?

    (A) corn   (C) microwave oven

    (B) information   (D) history

8 READ THINK EXPLAIN

Why did Josh and Elena keep their hands away from the steam when they opened the bag? Use information and details from the article to explain your answer.

_____

_____

_____

_____

_____

_____

_____

STOP

© Harcourt

FCAT Writing

Light and electricity are very important in our lives. What would happen if you had no lights or electricity for twenty-four hours? Write a story about what you would do if you had to live without electricity for a day.

Plan and write your story on separate sheets of paper.

This checklist shows you what your writing must have to receive your best score.

Checklist

I will earn my best score if:

➪ My story has a beginning, a middle, and an end.

➪ I explain what I do after losing electricity.

➪ I use details and examples that show what I do and how I feel.

➪ I use words that make my meaning clear, and I do not use the same words over and over.

➪ I use sentences that are complete.

➪ I make sure that all my words are spelled correctly.

     Grade 3

Read the article "How to Make a Cat Bed."
Then answer Numbers 1 through 5.

How to Make a Cat Bed

Most cats will sleep almost anywhere. They will curl up on your favorite chair, on a pile of newspapers, or even in your laundry basket. However, if you would like to make a special bed for your cat, you will find it easy to do.

First, you need to find a good <u>base</u> for the bed. A cardboard box or a wicker basket will work best. Next, fill the bed with soft cloth. Use old towels or a pillow that you don't use anymore. Then, add cat toys, catnip, and other things your cat likes. Most cats really like things that smell like their owners. An old shirt will work well.

Finally, find a good place for your cat's bed. Most cats prefer to be in high places. Mount the bed on a crate or another kind of stand.

Show the bed to your cat. Don't be disappointed if the cat doesn't use the bed at first. The cat may need to get used to the new bed before it decides to sleep there.

TEST-TAKING TIP
Pay attention to words that tell order, like *first*.

1 This article is mostly about

(A) how much cats sleep.

(B) what to do with an old shirt.

(C) how to make a place for your cat to sleep.

(D) how to care for your pets.

2 In this article, which word means the same as *base*?

(F) low   (H) sack

(G) guitar   (I) bottom

TEST-TAKING TIP
Don't be confused by words with more than one meaning. Read the sentences around the word to see how the word is used. Then, read the possible answers, and choose the best one.

Go On

© Harcourt

3 To make a cat bed, what is the first thing you must do?

Ⓐ find an old shirt

Ⓑ get a box or basket

Ⓒ put towels or a pillow on the bed

Ⓓ put the bed in a high place

TEST-TAKING TIP

Skim the article for the word *first*. Then read to find the answer to the question.

4 Why did the author write this article?

Ⓕ to convince people to buy cats

Ⓖ to tell how much she loves her cat

Ⓗ to help people make their cats more comfortable

Ⓘ to explain what kind of food cats prefer

TEST-TAKING TIP

Some of the answers tell about things that don't appear in the selection. Cross them out. Then decide which answer tells what the article is mostly about.

5 What are the steps to making a cat bed? Tell them in order.

READ
THINK
EXPLAIN

_____

_____

_____

_____

_____

_____

_____

Go On

Grade 3

Name _____

Read the ad for the sale at Pet World. Then answer Numbers 6 through 11.

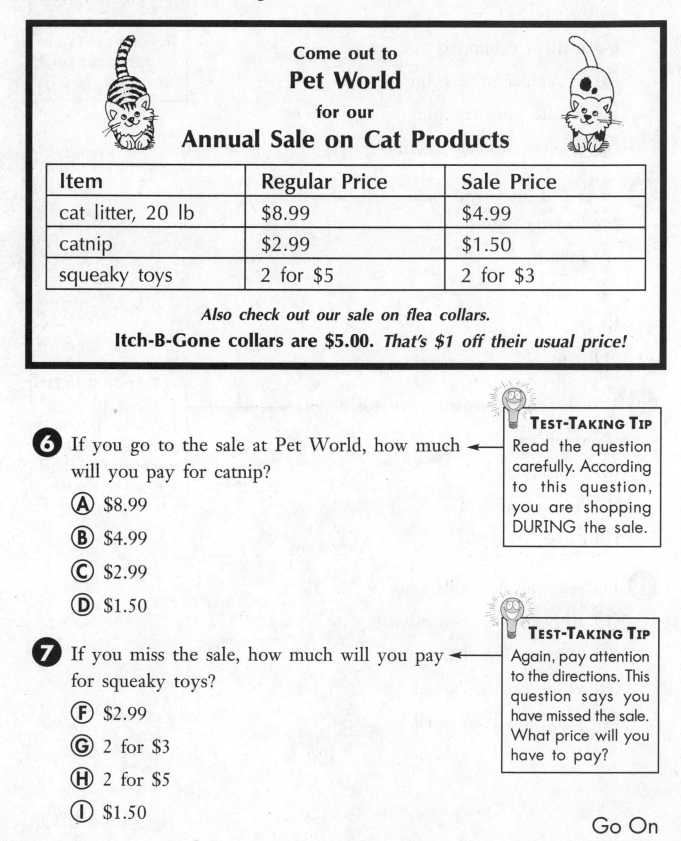

Come out to
Pet World
for our
Annual Sale on Cat Products

Item	Regular Price	Sale Price
cat litter, 20 lb	$8.99	$4.99
catnip	$2.99	$1.50
squeaky toys	2 for $5	2 for $3

Also check out our sale on flea collars.
Itch-B-Gone collars are $5.00. *That's $1 off their usual price!*

6 If you go to the sale at Pet World, how much will you pay for catnip?

Ⓐ $8.99

Ⓑ $4.99

Ⓒ $2.99

Ⓓ $1.50

TEST-TAKING TIP
Read the question carefully. According to this question, you are shopping DURING the sale.

7 If you miss the sale, how much will you pay for squeaky toys?

Ⓕ $2.99

Ⓖ 2 for $3

Ⓗ 2 for $5

Ⓘ $1.50

TEST-TAKING TIP
Again, pay attention to the directions. This question says you have missed the sale. What price will you have to pay?

Go On

Lesson 6

8 If you added the information about flea collars to the chart, where would you say that Itch-B-Gone collars are $5?

    A in item column

    B in regular price column

    C in sale price column

    D in an additional column

9 In the ad, the word *annual* tells you that cat products go on sale

    F monthly.

    G weekly.

    H yearly.

    I daily.

10 Which product usually sells for $8.99?

    A cat litter

    B squeaky toys

    C flea collars

    D catnip

11 On sale, the flea collars are

    F 50 cents less than usual.

    G 75 cents less than usual.

    H $1.00 less than usual.

    I $2.00 less than usual.

STOP

Grade 3

Amaya went fishing with her grandfather, her uncle, and her brother. Read the story "Peanut Butter Bait." Then answer Numbers 1 through 8.

Peanut Butter Bait

One day last summer, Grandpa Benner and Uncle Henry took Owen and me fishing. We went out on the lake in a rowboat. Grandpa Benner said we should use worms as bait to catch fish. He showed us how to attach a worm to a fishing hook. I attached a worm the same way Grandpa showed me, but Owen didn't.

"Why aren't you putting a worm on your hook, Owen?" Grandpa asked.

"I don't want to hurt the worm," Owen said. ◄—

"Owen likes all kinds of crawly things," I explained. "I, personally, think they're creepy."

Uncle Henry had a box of plastic worms with him. "Owen, do you want to use a plastic worm instead?"

Owen looked at the plastic worms. "They don't look very tasty," he said. "I don't think the fish will like plastic."

Uncle Henry and Grandpa looked at each other and shrugged. "Do what you want, Owen," said Grandpa. "Can you think of something else that would work?"

Owen sat and thought for a minute. Then he ◄— opened his lunchbox and pinched off a corner of his peanut butter sandwich. He attached it to his hook and tossed the hook into the water. A few minutes later, Owen's line moved. There was a huge fish at the end of it. The peanut butter bait worked!

TEST-TAKING TIP
Pay attention when characters talk about their thoughts and feelings. You can learn a lot about them that way.

TEST-TAKING TIP
Remember that characters don't always share their ideas out loud. Owen doesn't answer Grandpa's question with words. Instead, his actions tell what he is thinking.

Go On

Now answer Numbers 1 through 8. Base your answers on the story "Peanut Butter Bait."

1 What would be another good title for this story? ◄

- Ⓐ "Grandpa Saves the Day"
- Ⓑ "Amaya's Surprise"
- Ⓒ "Owen's Great Idea"
- Ⓓ "Uncle Henry's Plastic Worms"

> **TEST-TAKING TIP**
> Titles usually hint at the main idea of a story. Read the answer choices. Which answer tells what the story is mostly about?

2 Who tells the story?

- Ⓕ Owen
- Ⓖ Grandpa
- Ⓗ Uncle Henry
- Ⓘ Amaya

3 What problem does Owen have? ◄

- Ⓐ He does not know how to fish.
- Ⓑ He is afraid of the water.
- Ⓒ He does not want to use the bait.
- Ⓓ He is tired.

> **TEST-TAKING TIP**
> Problems usually happen in the middle of a story. Look at the middle of the story again to find Owen's problem.

4 What does Uncle Henry suggest for Owen?

- Ⓕ He tells Owen to clean the boat.
- Ⓖ He tells Owen not to use bait.
- Ⓗ He gives Owen some other crawly things.
- Ⓘ He offers Owen a plastic worm.

Go On

Grade 3

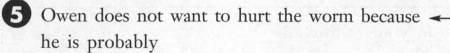

5 Owen does not want to hurt the worm because he is probably

   Ⓐ tired.

   Ⓑ afraid.

   Ⓒ kind.

   Ⓓ excited.

> **TEST-TAKING TIP**
> Use what you know about people to answer this question. What kind of person does not want to hurt a worm? Choose the best answer.

6 This selection is an example of

   Ⓕ fiction.

   Ⓖ nonfiction.

   Ⓗ persuasive writing.

   Ⓘ poetry.

> **TEST-TAKING TIP**
> Use what you know about different kinds of writing to answer this question. Cross out the answers that you know are wrong. Then choose the best answer.

7 How does Owen solve his problem?

_____

_____

_____

_____

_____

_____

_____

_____

Go On

8 Retell this story in your own words.

READ
THINK
EXPLAIN

_____

_____

_____

_____

_____

_____

_____

_____

_____

_____

_____

_____

STOP

Read the article "Elephants and Their Trunks."
Then answer Numbers 1 through 6.

Elephants and Their Trunks

The African elephant is the largest living land animal.
It stands 10-13 feet tall at the shoulder and weighs
up to 8 tons. The Indian elephant is shorter, weighs
less, and has smaller ears than the African elephant.
The two animals have one thing in common that no
other animal has: a trunk. The trunk is a very long
nose, which can do much more than just help the
elephant smell.

The trunk is used for breathing, eating, and
drinking. The elephant uses the tip of its trunk to
pick grasses, leaves, and fruit for food. Then it places
the food in its mouth. An elephant drinks by sucking
water into its trunk. Then it squirts the water into
its mouth.

> **TEST-TAKING TIP**
> Underline words or phrases that show comparison or contrast. This will help you find information quickly if you need to refer to it.

1 From the title, you know that this story will be about

   (A) water.   (C) fruit.

   (B) India.   (D) elephants.

2 How is an Indian elephant different from an African elephant?

   (F) The Indian elephant has smaller eyes.

   (G) The Indian elephant has smaller ears.

   (H) The Indian elephant has smaller feet.

   (I) The Indian elephant has smaller tusks.

Go On

3 Elephants use their trunks for all of these EXCEPT

Ⓐ eating.

Ⓑ sleeping.

Ⓒ drinking.

Ⓓ breathing.

4 This passage probably comes from a ◄

Ⓕ textbook.

Ⓖ biography.

Ⓗ letter.

Ⓘ interview.

> **TEST-TAKING TIP**
> Use what you know about different styles of writing to answer this question.

5 What is the purpose of this passage? ◄

Ⓐ to tell a funny story about elephants

Ⓑ to describe the Indian elephant

Ⓒ to explain the characteristics of elephants

Ⓓ to convince people that elephants are large animals

> **TEST-TAKING TIP**
> Think about why the author wrote the passage.

6 The writer compares the African elephant and the Indian elephant to show that they both have

Ⓕ a trunk.

Ⓖ ears.

Ⓗ teeth.

Ⓘ toes.

© Harcourt

Go On

Grade 3

Name _____

Read the article "They're Not Gold at All."
Then answer Numbers 7 through 11.

TEST-TAKING TIP
Always read the title of the story. The title often tells you the main idea of the story.

They're Not Gold at All

TEST-TAKING TIP
Here in the first paragraph you discover that goldfish come in many colors.

Have you ever looked carefully at a tank of goldfish? If you have, then you know that many goldfish are not gold at all. In fact, goldfish come in lots of different colors. In the wild, most goldfish are olive green. Their color helps them hide in plants that live in ponds and rivers. When goldfish don't live in the wild, they may have brighter colors. Many turn golden red. Some goldfish are completely white or silver. Other goldfish have spots on them that are a different color from the rest of their bodies. They are called calicoes because they have many colors, just like a calico cat.

Goldfish also come in different shapes and sizes. Most goldfish are very small, but some grow to be one foot long! One type of goldfish has a big head and bulging eyes. It is called a telescope fish. Another kind of goldfish is the fantail fish. It has two tails instead of one!

7 What is the FIRST paragraph mostly about?

Ⓐ Goldfish come in many sizes.

Ⓑ Goldfish come in many colors.

Ⓒ Goldfish come in many shapes.

Ⓓ Goldfish have interesting eyes.

© Harcourt

Go On

Lesson 8

8 Which sentence *supports* the main idea of the first paragraph?

    F In the wild, most goldfish are olive green.

    G Have you ever looked carefully at a tank of goldfish?

    H Some have big heads and bulging eyes.

    I Another kind of goldfish is called the fantail fish.

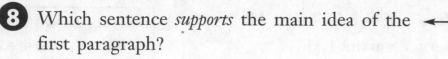

TEST-TAKING TIP

Supporting statements always appear in the paragraph of the idea they support. Some of these answers do not appear in the first paragraph. Cross them out to help you narrow your choices.

9 How is the fantail fish different from other goldfish?

    A It is larger than other goldfish.

    B It has two tails.

    C It lives only in rivers.

    D It is silver.

10 Why do goldfish who do not live in the wild often have brighter colors?

    F The goldfish don't need to hide from enemies.

    G Bright colors are pretty.

    H The food that the fish eat gives them bright colors.

    I Bright colors help the fish swim faster.

TEST-TAKING TIP

To answer this question, think about the disadvantage of being colorful. Why would being colorful be a problem for a fish in the wild?

11 How is the telescope fish unlike other goldfish?

READ
THINK
EXPLAIN

_____

_____

_____

_____

© Harcourt

STOP

Grade 3

Lesson 9

Read the story "Train Ride." Then answer Numbers 1 through 5.

Train Ride

Julio couldn't believe he was finally on a train! He had seen many trains, but he had never been inside a train until now. He and his mom were going to New Orleans to see his cousins.

When he was waiting on the platform, Julio had seen people sitting in the dining car. "Mom, will we get to eat in the dining car?" Julio asked.

"Yes, in a little while," Mom answered.

The train <u>lurched</u> forward, and Julio used his hands to steady himself. The conductor came and asked for his ticket. Julio handed it to him and smiled. He knew this trip would be a great adventure!

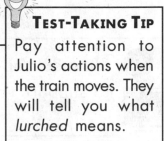

TEST-TAKING TIP
Pay attention to Julio's actions when the train moves. They will tell you what *lurched* means.

1 Why is Julio taking a train ride?

Ⓐ He wants to see a baseball game.

Ⓑ He is going to visit family.

Ⓒ He needs to go to school.

Ⓓ The bus broke down.

2 Who is Julio traveling with?

Ⓕ his mother

Ⓖ his father

Ⓗ a friend

Ⓘ the conductor

TEST-TAKING TIP
It might be tempting to say that Julio is traveling with the conductor. But Julio and the conductor will see each other only a few times. Who is Julio spending most of his travel time with?

Go On

3 What part of the train is Julio most interested in?

Ⓐ the sleeping car

Ⓑ the dining car

Ⓒ the engine

Ⓓ the whistle

TEST-TAKING TIP
Which part of the train does Julio say he wants to visit?

4 What does the word *lurched* mean?

Ⓕ rolled

Ⓖ jumped

Ⓗ slid

Ⓘ leaned

TEST-TAKING TIP
What kind of motion causes you to steady yourself with your hands, as Julio did?

5 How do you think Julio feels at the end of the story? Give details to support your answer.

READ
THINK
EXPLAIN

_____

_____

_____

_____

_____

_____

_____

© Harcourt

Go On

Grade 3

Read the story "Working on the Railroad."
Then answer Numbers 6 through 11.

Working on the Railroad

Charles drove another <u>spike</u> into the ground. Then he stood up and wiped his brow. As far as he could see to the east or west, miles of railroad track stretched across the land.

Like many young men in 1869, Charles was helping to build a railroad line that would connect the eastern United States with the western United States. All day long he drove metal spikes into the ground to keep the rails in place. It was <u>backbreaking</u> work. ◄

It was also very exciting. Very soon the final spike would be nailed into the ground. Then this big country would seem like a much smaller place.

> **TEST-TAKING TIP**
> The word *backbreaking* is an exaggeration. What image does it create in your mind? What do you think it actually means?

6 Charles wipes his brow because ◄

   Ⓐ he is hot.

   Ⓑ he is hungry.

   Ⓒ a bug landed on his brow.

   Ⓓ he feels sick.

> **TEST-TAKING TIP**
> To answer this question, think about the last time you wiped your brow. Why did you do it?

7 A spike is probably like a

   Ⓕ hammer.   Ⓗ nail.

   Ⓖ saw.   Ⓘ rake.

8 What does *backbreaking* mean?

   Ⓐ long   Ⓒ difficult and tiring

   Ⓑ fun and easy   Ⓓ quiet

Go On

9 The railroad will connect

TEST-TAKING TIP
You can look back at the story to find the answer to this question.

(F) north and south.

(G) the eastern and western parts of the United States.

(H) North America and South America.

(I) the United States and Canada.

10 Which answer choice will be one effect of the railroad?

TEST-TAKING TIP
To answer this question, look back at the story. Remind yourself where the railroad travels.

(A) People can travel to Canada easily.

(B) People can cross the United States more quickly.

(C) People will prefer horses and buggies to trains.

(D) People will never use cars.

11 How is Charles's adventure different from Julio's? Use details from the stories to support your answer.

READ
THINK
EXPLAIN

_____

_____

_____

_____

_____

_____

_____

STOP

© Harcourt

Read the story "Maki Visits the Empire State Building." Then answer Numbers 1 through 8.

Maki Visits the Empire State Building

Maki was so excited! She and her grandfather were on their way up one of the tallest buildings in the world! It was the Empire State Building.

After a long ride, the elevator stopped at the 86th floor. Maki and her grandfather stepped out of the elevator. They were on the viewing deck, where people can look out at the city below.

Maki looked around at New York City. Grandpa showed her lots of interesting buildings. He pointed to the Chrysler Building, which was very shiny. Then he pointed to Madison Square Garden, where his favorite basketball team plays. He also told her the names of the two rivers she could see. They were the East River and the Hudson River.

Maki found a telescope on the viewing deck. She looked through the telescope. She could see the Statue of Liberty far away.

The wind <u>whipped</u> Maki's hair all around. She walked around the viewing deck. She looked at the tall buildings and the ocean. She knew that there was another viewing deck on the 102nd floor, the top floor of the building. She wondered how everything would look from there.

TEST-TAKING TIP
The first paragraph gives important information about the Empire State Building.

TEST-TAKING TIP
Whipped has several different meanings. Look back at the sentence to see how it is used in this story.

© Harcourt

Go On

Name _____

Now answer Numbers 1–8. Base your answers on the story "Maki Visits the Empire State Building."

1 What will Maki probably do next?

Ⓐ go to the park

Ⓑ go home for supper

Ⓒ go to the 102nd floor

Ⓓ go to a movie

TEST-TAKING TIP Recall what you know about Maki and how she feels about her experience. What would you do?

2 What part of the story supports your answer to Number 1?

Ⓕ The elevator ride was long.

Ⓖ Maki looked around at New York City.

Ⓗ She wondered how everything would look from there.

Ⓘ Grandpa showed her lots of interesting buildings.

TEST-TAKING TIP Which answer choice reflects Maki's curiosity?

3 READ THINK EXPLAIN

Based on the story, why might the Empire State Building provide tourists like Maki with telescopes and viewing areas?

_____

_____

_____

_____

_____

_____

_____

© Harcourt

Go On

Grade 3

4 What does the word *whipped* mean in the story?

    (F) mixed   (H) washed

    (G) blew   (I) curled

5 A good word to describe Maki is ◀─────

    (A) afraid.   (C) grumpy.

    (B) curious.   (D) unfriendly.

> **TEST-TAKING TIP**
> The story doesn't use any of these words to describe Maki. Remember what Maki thinks and how she acts. Then pick the best answer.

6 Through the telescope, Maki sees ◀─────

    (F) two rivers.

    (G) her house.

    (H) the Statue of Liberty.

    (I) the Chrysler Building.

> **TEST-TAKING TIP**
> Maki can see several of these things from the viewing deck. Which one does she see through a TELESCOPE?

7 What happened right AFTER Maki stepped off the elevator?

    (A) She found a telescope.

    (B) The wind whipped her hair.

    (C) Grandpa showed her lots of buildings.

    (D) She saw the Statue of Liberty.

8 This story is mostly about

    (F) visiting an interesting place.

    (G) two beautiful rivers.

    (H) buildings where sports teams play.

    (I) Grandpa's friendship with Maki.

STOP

FCAT Writing

What was your community like one hundred years ago?
Think about what people wore, what kinds of work they did,
and how they traveled. Think about how things looked, sounded,
and smelled. Then write a composition that explains what your
community was like one hundred years ago.

Plan and write your composition on separate sheets of paper.

This checklist shows you what your writing must have to receive
your best score.

Checklist

I will earn my best score if:

⇨ My explanation tells what my community was like one hundred
years ago.

⇨ I use details and examples to show how things looked, sounded, felt,
and smelled.

⇨ I use interesting words that make my meaning clear.

⇨ My sentences are varied and complete.

⇨ I use commas, quotations, and end punctuation correctly.

© Harcourt

Read the article "Mr. Lopez Joins Jollyville."
Then answer Numbers 1 through 6.

Mr. Lopez Joins Jollyville

There's a new face at Jollyville Elementary School
this year. It's Mr. José Lopez! Mr. Lopez teaches one
of the third-grade classes. He is taking over for Mrs.
Hopkins because she retired. ◄

When Mr. Lopez was young, he used to play
school with his brothers. Mr. Lopez always played
the teacher. He gave his brothers homework. Then
he corrected the homework and gave it back. Mr.
Lopez thinks those games made him want to teach.

Mr. Lopez says his favorite subject is reading.
He loves to read stories and help other people learn
to read. Every day at two o'clock, many students sit
on the floor in Mr. Lopez's room. That's when he
has story time. Then they have a reading lesson.

Mr. Lopez has a wife named Annette and a baby
son named Emilio. He also has a dog named Paws. You
can meet them all at the school picnic next weekend.

TEST-TAKING TIP
As you read, pay attention to the reasons that things happen. Why did Mr. Lopez take over the third-grade class?

1 Look at the outline in the chart. Decide which ◄
topic belongs beside the number III.

I.	Mr. Lopez's job at school
II.	Growing up
III.	
IV.	Family

TEST-TAKING TIP
The chart uses Roman numerals instead of numbers. The numeral III refers to the number 3. Which paragraph do you think you should you look at to answer the question?

Ⓐ Pets   Ⓒ Hobbies

Ⓑ Favorite subject   Ⓓ Favorite foods

Go On

© Harcourt

2 Why did Mr. Lopez take over for Mrs. Hopkins?

Ⓕ She moved away.　Ⓗ She had a baby.

Ⓖ She got sick.　Ⓘ She retired.

TEST-TAKING TIP
If you don't remember why Mr. Lopez had to take over, look back at the story to find out.

When does Mr. Lopez's class have story time?

Ⓐ at noon　　　Ⓒ at two o'clock

Ⓑ at one o'clock　Ⓓ at three o'clock

4 Where can you meet Mr. Lopez's dog, Paws?

Ⓕ in his classroom

Ⓖ in the schoolyard

Ⓗ at the school picnic

Ⓘ at the school play

According to the story, what did Mr. Lopez play when he was young?

Ⓐ soccer　　　Ⓒ baseball

Ⓑ tag　　　　Ⓓ school

6 What made Mr. Lopez want to teach?

READ
THINK
EXPLAIN

_____

_____

_____

_____

_____

_____

_____

Go On

Grade 3

Name _____

Read the play "New Girl in Town."
Then answer Numbers 7 through 11.

New Girl in Town

It is the first day of the school year. A girl gets on the school bus. She looks for a seat.

Kayla: Can I sit here?

Anya: Sure. I'm Anya. What's your name?

Kayla: I'm Kayla. I just moved here from Arizona.

Anya: That's far away. Isn't that where the Grand Canyon is?

Kayla: Yes, I went there last summer. A tour guide led us down to the canyon bottom on donkeys!

Anya: Really? That must have been great! Come with me when we get to school. I'll introduce you to my friends. Then you can tell them about your trip, too.

Kayla: Okay! I'm so glad I met you.

7 How are Anya and Kayla alike?

   Ⓕ They have the same friends.

   Ⓖ They both think the Grand Canyon is interesting.

   Ⓗ They both have moved to a new place.

   Ⓘ They both think donkeys are stubborn.

8 Why does Kayla speak to Anya?

   Ⓐ Kayla needs a place to sit on the bus.

   Ⓑ Kayla picked up Anya's book.

   Ⓒ Kayla wanted to talk about her new school.

   Ⓓ Kayla forgot to write down the homework assignment.

TEST-TAKING TIP
Read the material in italics carefully. It tells WHAT happens in the selection and WHERE it happens.

TEST-TAKING TIP
Look at the answer choices carefully. Which ones are not supported by the reading? Cross them out. Then look back at the text to help you choose the best remaining answer.

TEST-TAKING TIP
Skim the beginning of the dialogue to find the answer to this question.

Go On

© Harcourt

Lesson 11

51

9 The theme of this selection is ◄————

    F playing by the rules.

    G learning a new skill.

    H starting over in a new place.

    I growing up.

> **TEST-TAKING TIP**
> A *theme* is the main idea of a story, poem, or play. Which answer tells the main idea of this selection?

10 Do you think that it is easier to read plays than fiction? Support your opinion with details from the play.

READ
THINK
EXPLAIN

_____

_____

_____

_____

_____

11 Tell how Kayla is like Mr. Lopez.

READ
THINK
EXPLAIN

_____

_____

_____

_____

_____

STOP

Grade 3

© Harcourt

Read the article "Silly-Sounding Laws."
Then answer Numbers 1 through 8.

Silly-Sounding Laws

Since the early days of our country, many laws have been passed. Some laws make communities safer places. It's no surprise, then, that highways have speed limits and that robbery is against the law.

However, in Winnetka, Illinois, there is a law against removing your shoes in a theater if your feet smell. Did you know that in New Jersey, you can't slurp soup in public places? These laws sound funny, but they really do exist.

Every state has laws that may have made sense once but now are outdated. In Reed City, Michigan, for example, it's <u>illegal</u> to own both a cat and a bird. In Louisiana you aren't allowed to whistle on Sunday. In North Carolina it's illegal to drink water or milk on a train.

How did these laws come about? We do know that many of them came from England. Other laws were based on religious beliefs. Others were created in times of emergency. When the emergency ended, the law remained.

Why are some silly-sounding laws still around? Often, it's easier to leave a law in place than to go through the legal steps to remove it. Even though many of these outdated laws remain, few of them are <u>enforced</u>.

We're not the only country with strange laws. In London, England, it's against the law to kiss in a movie theater. People in Finland must be able to read to get married. A guide dog is the only kind of dog allowed in Iceland.

TEST-TAKING TIP
When you see the word *however*, pay attention. It tells you that the writer's message is about to turn in a different direction.

TEST-TAKING TIP
To decide what *enforced* means, read the whole sentence. It will give you clues.

Go On

© Harcourt

Every year new laws are passed. Others either are removed or not enforced. Just in case, though, be careful not to fish from the back of a giraffe in Idaho!

Now answer Numbers 1 through 8. Base your answers on the article "Silly-Sounding Laws."

1 Which of these is the best summary for this article?

(A) Many states have outdated and strange laws.

(B) The United States has traffic laws.

(C) All laws should be enforced.

(D) Laws are made to make life difficult.

2 What is the main idea of the third paragraph? ◄—

(F) We should never break a law.

(G) Whistling is hard to do on Sunday.

(H) Every state has laws that are outdated.

(I) Some laws were based on religious beliefs.

> **TEST-TAKING TIP**
> Read the directions carefully. Then make sure you reread the right paragraph.

3 According to the article, how did we get some of our laws?

(A) from encyclopedias

(B) from the southwestern United States

(C) from England

(D) from the 1920s

4 What does the word *illegal* mean in this article? ◄—

(F) agreed upon

(G) enforced by the people

(H) against the law

(I) unwell

> **TEST-TAKING TIP**
> Break the word *illegal* into syllables. Look at the prefix *il-*. Think about what the prefix means and how it changes the meaning of the word *legal*.

© Harcourt

Go On

Grade 3

5 According to the article, why are some silly-sounding laws still around?

READ
THINK
EXPLAIN

_____

_____

_____

_____

 6 What are some reasons that these laws were created? Support your answer with details from the article.

READ
THINK
EXPLAIN

_____

_____

_____

_____

_____

 7 Why might someone pass laws like those in Winnetka, Illinois, and the state of New Jersey?

READ
THINK
EXPLAIN

_____

_____

_____

_____

Go On

Lesson 12

Name _____

8 What might be the purpose of the last paragraph? Explain your answer.

STOP

Grade 3

Read the story "Jonah's Surprise." Then answer Numbers 1 through 6.

Jonah's Surprise

Jonah's Aunt Maria was waiting for him when Jonah's dad drove up to the farmhouse.

"Jonah!" Maria cried. "Come with me! I have a big surprise for you!"

Jonah followed Maria through the house. The whole house smelled like fresh-baked apple pie.

"Mmmmmm! Apple pie!" Jonah said. "Is that the surprise?"

"Nope! Come this way," said Maria.

Jonah followed Maria out to the barn. Inside, Jonah saw a calf curled up on the ground. She had <u>soft</u> brown eyes, and her brown coat was wet and gleaming.

"She was just born today," Maria said. "I want you to name her. That's your surprise!"

> **TEST-TAKING TIP**
> When people talk to family or friends, they often use informal language. *Nope* is an informal version of *No*.

> **TEST-TAKING TIP**
> Some words have more than one meaning. How can eyes be *soft*?

1 Why did the author write this story?

Ⓐ to convince you to visit a farm

Ⓑ to teach you about calves

Ⓒ to share a suspenseful tale

Ⓓ to explain how to make apple pie

2 Next, Jonah will probably

Ⓕ eat apple pie.

Ⓖ go back home.

Ⓗ name the calf.

Ⓘ go to the park.

Go On

© Harcourt

3 In this story, *soft* means the same as ←

    A gentle   **C** loud

    B smooth   **D** wide

> **TEST-TAKING TIP**
> Look back at the story to see how *soft* is used in a sentence. Then pick the best answer.

4 From the story, you can tell that Maria is

    F thoughtful.   **H** angry.

    G obedient.   **I** shy.

5 Why does Jonah say "Mmmmmm"? ←

    A He likes apple pie.

    B He is confused.

    C He wants a glass of water.

    D He hopes Maria will slow down.

> **TEST-TAKING TIP**
> *Mmmmmm* is a made-up word. It stands for a sound. When do people make the sound *Mmmmmm*?

6 Why do you think Maria wants Jonah to name the calf? Have you ever done something for that reason? Use details to support your answer.

READ
THINK
EXPLAIN

_____

_____

_____

_____

_____

_____

Go On

© Harcourt

Name _____

Read the poem "The Rooster Who Overslept."
Then answer Numbers 7 through 12.

The Rooster Who Overslept

There once was a rooster named Joe

who never woke early to <u>crow</u>. ◄

When the sun rose,

Joe continued to doze

although he sure wished it weren't so!

Joe knew a goose named Suze Purty ◄

who woke up each day at five-thirty.

Joe said, "Wake me, sweet Suze!

Then I'll sing great cockle-doos

and be a more helpful old birdy!"

TEST-TAKING TIP
Notice the word *crow*. Sometimes the word *crow* refers to a bird. Here *crow* is being used as an action word.

TEST-TAKING TIP
How should you say the word *Suze*? Remember that the final *e* on a word is often silent and that a silent *e* gives the other vowel a long sound.

TEST-TAKING TIP
Look at the title and the first few lines to answer this question.

7 What is Joe's problem? ◄

  (F) He never crows at dawn.

  (G) He doesn't like farm life.

  (H) He can't sing.

  (I) He is forgetful.

8 Joe wants to

  (A) be a goose.   (C) do his job well.

  (B) chase chickens.   (D) make friends.

Go On

9 Which word BEST describes Suze Purty?

F lazy   **H** active

G angry   **I** intelligent

10 In the poem, Joe is a

A hen.   **C** sparrow.

B goose.   **D** rooster.

11 The OPPOSITE of *doze* is ◄

F sleep.

G wake up.

H clean.

I sing.

TEST-TAKING TIP
Read the directions carefully. Notice that they ask you to choose the OPPOSITE of *doze* instead of the definition.

12 How will Joe's problem be solved?

READ
THINK
EXPLAIN

_____

_____

_____

_____

_____

_____

_____

© Harcourt

STOP

Read the article "Tara Lipinski: Figure Skating Champion." Then answer Numbers 1 through 8.

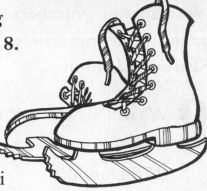

Tara Lipinski: Figure Skating Champion

By the time she was three years old, Tara Lipinski was roller-skating. When she was six, she started taking ice-skating lessons. By the time she was twelve years old, she won a silver medal in the national junior championships.

A silver medal is good, but not as good as a gold medal. Only skaters in the senior championships got gold medals. So Tara became a senior skater the next year. She placed third in the country!

The best part about winning third place was that Tara could skate in the world championships.

Figure skaters compete by skating two programs. The first has many <u>difficult</u> moves, such as jumps and spins. The second program has moves that are hard to do, but it also shows the skater's grace.

At the world championships, Tara finished in fifteenth place.

The next year went very well for Tara, and she won the national title. Tara went on to win the world title. At fourteen years of age, she was the youngest person ever to win a world gold medal in figure skating.

Then it was time for the Winter Olympics. When Tara Lipinski skated that night, she was like a firecracker. The crowd was on its feet, cheering. A few minutes later, they were on their feet again. Tara had won! At fifteen years of age, she was the youngest figure skater ever to win an Olympic gold medal.

TEST-TAKING TIP
Don't try to remember the names of all the championships Tara competed in. If you need to answer a question about one, you can look back at the article later if you need to. Notice that each time Tara competes, she competes at a higher level.

TEST-TAKING TIP
Pay attention to facts that set Tara apart from other skaters.

Go On

© Harcourt

Now answer Numbers 1 through 8. Base your answers on the article "Tara Lipinski: Figure Skating Champion."

1 What does the word *difficult* mean in this article?

Ⓐ beautiful

Ⓑ hard to do

Ⓒ short

Ⓓ large

2 How did Tara probably feel after skating at the Winter Olympics?

Ⓕ excited and proud

Ⓖ that she hadn't skated her best

Ⓗ afraid that she would lose

Ⓘ ready to go home

> **TEST-TAKING TIP**
> The article doesn't tell how Tara felt. Look back at the story to see how Tara skated at the Winter Olympics. How do you think she felt?

3 Tara Lipinski won a silver medal in the

Ⓐ junior championships.

Ⓑ senior championships.

Ⓒ world championships.

Ⓓ regional championships.

> **TEST-TAKING TIP**
> Tara competed in a lot of different championships. Look back at the article to see when she won her silver medal.

Go On

Grade 3

4 What was Tara Lipinski's first achievement?

(F) She placed third in the country.

(G) She won a silver medal in the National Junior Championships.

(H) She finished fifteenth in the world championships.

(I) She won an Olympic gold medal.

5 What happened the year after Tara Lipinski skated in her first world championship?

(A) She retired.

(B) She won a bronze medal.

(C) She won the national title.

(D) She won a gold medal at the Olympics.

6 This article is mostly about

(F) the Winter Olympics.

(G) a champion ice skater.

(H) a girl made from gold.

(I) roller-skating.

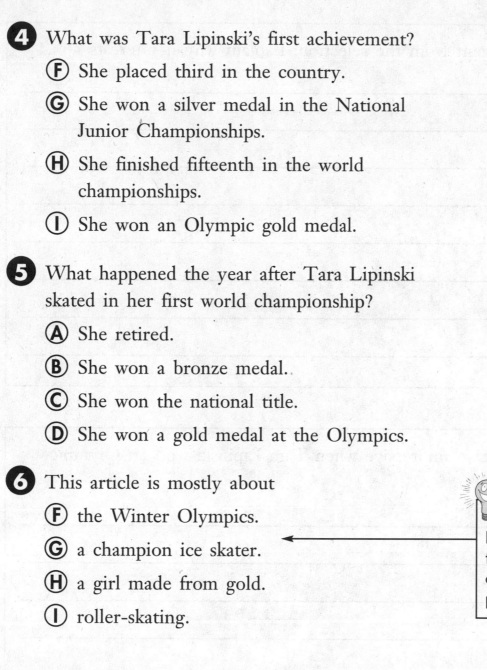

TEST-TAKING TIP
Look for the answer that is the topic of most of the paragraphs.

© Harcourt

Go On

7 Retell an event from the selection. Explain why it interests you.

READ
THINK
EXPLAIN

_____

_____

_____

_____

_____

_____

8 Why was it so impressive when Tara Lipinski won an Olympic gold medal?

READ
THINK
EXPLAIN

_____

_____

_____

_____

_____

_____

STOP

Grade 3

**Read the article "Old and New Lighthouses."
Then answer Numbers 1 through 8.**

Old and New Lighthouses

Lighthouses have protected ships along the coasts all over the world. For thousands of years they have kept ships from sailing too close to rocky shores.

Some early lighthouses burned wood or coal in metal braziers, or baskets. Others used large candles to make lights for the ships. Later, oil-burning lamps were used.

Today, electricity is used in most lighthouses. Some <u>unpiloted</u> lighthouses even use sunlight to make electricity for the lights.

Most lighthouses use a flashing light to warn ships. Each lighthouse uses a different pattern of flashes. This helps a ship identify the lighthouse it is nearing.

Lighthouses are built of many different materials. Some must be built stronger than others. A lighthouse built on land does not need to be as strong as one that is built on a small, rocky island. Island lighthouses have to be very strong to stand up against strong waves.

In the United States today, many lighthouses work without keepers. The signal lights come on automatically at night. In fog, lighthouses also send out <u>signal</u> noises to warn ships that may not be able to see the signal lights.

TEST-TAKING TIP
Another unusual word is *unpiloted*. One way to figure out what this word means is to look at the parts of the word. Think about what a *pilot* does. What do you think it means to *pilot* a lighthouse? Then think about where you have seen the prefix *un-* before. What happens when you add *un-* to the word *pilot*?

TEST-TAKING TIP
As you read, pay attention to the ways some lighthouses are different from others.

© Harcourt

Go On

Now answer Numbers 1 through 8. Base your answers on the article "Old and New Lighthouses."

1) How long have ships relied on lighthouses to warn them about rocks?

(A) ten years

(B) one hundred years

(C) five hundred years

(D) thousands of years

TEST-TAKING TIP
The article talks about old lighthouses before it talks about new ones. It makes sense to reread the beginning of the article to see for how long lighthouses have been used.

2 What does the word *signal* mean in this article?

(F) shipping   (H) warning

(G) building   (I) reaching

TEST-TAKING TIP
This word can be used in two different ways. Find the underlined word in the story. Then replace it with each answer choice to find which one is correct.

3) What does the word *unpiloted* mean in this article?

(A) without people

(B) with one person

(C) with four people

(D) with ten people

4 Some lighthouses use sunlight to make

(F) fires.   (H) coals.

(G) electricity.   (I) candles.

5) Many lighthouses today do not have

(A) keepers.

(B) lights.

(C) horns.

(D) rocks around them.

Go On

Grade 3

© Harcourt

6 What first replaced fires in lighthouses?

(F) oil lamps   (H) coal

(G) sunlight   (I) torches

TEST-TAKING TIP
Over the years, several things have replaced fires in lighthouses. Read carefully to find the FIRST thing to replace fires.

7 Why does the writer contrast lighthouses built on land to lighthouses built on rocky islands?

(A) to convince readers that lighthouses built on land are better

(B) to show why lighthouses built on rocky islands must be stronger

(C) to show how lighthouses on land use electricity

(D) to show how lighthouses on rocky islands send signals

TEST-TAKING TIP
Several of the answer choices describe things that lighthouses do. Be sure to pick the one that answers the question correctly.

8 According to the article, how do lighthouses warn ships on foggy nights?

READ
THINK
EXPLAIN

_____

_____

_____

_____

_____

_____

_____

© Harcourt

STOP

Lesson 15   67

FCAT Writing

Everyone appreciates a good neighbor. What makes someone a good neighbor? What special things does a good neighbor do? Write an essay that explains how good neighbors make the community a better place for everyone.

Plan and write your essay on separate sheets of paper.

This checklist shows what your writing must have to receive your best score.

Checklist

I will earn my best score if:

⇨ My essay has a beginning, a middle, and an end.

⇨ My essay tells what makes a good neighbor.

⇨ I use details to show what good neighbors do.

⇨ I use words that make my meaning clear, and I do not use the same words over and over.

⇨ Each sentence and proper name begins with a capital letter.

⇨ Each sentence ends with a period, an exclamation point, or a question mark.

© Harcourt

Read the article "Kettledrums." Then answer Numbers 1 through 6.

Kettledrums

A kettledrum is a kind of drum with a skin stretched over a large shell. The shell is in the shape of a bowl. The skin is held tightly in several different ways. It may be held by screws or may be tied on with a narrow strip of leather.

Kettledrums are usually played in pairs. Each one has a different pitch, which means that the musical tone of one kettledrum is higher or lower than the other. One person plays both drums. It is believed that the kettledrum was first used in the Middle East. From there, its use spread through Africa, Asia, and Europe.

1 What is the first paragraph mostly about?

A how kettledrums are played

B how kettledrums are made

C instruments from the Middle East

D large shells

2 This article is full of facts. A name for writing that tells facts is

F fiction.

G nonfiction.

H poetry.

I drama.

Go On

When a person plays a pair of kettledrums, how are the drums different from each other?

(A) They are different colors.

(B) They have different pitches.

(C) One makes loud sounds, and the other makes soft sounds.

(D) One is made of steel, and the other is made of leather.

Kettledrums were first used in

(F) Africa.

(H) Europe.

(G) Asia.

(I) the Middle East.

5 The part of the kettledrum a drummer hits is made of

(A) paper.

(C) plastic.

(B) cloth.

(D) skin.

6 Write a summary of the article in your own words.

READ
THINK
EXPLAIN

_____

_____

_____

_____

_____

_____

_____

© Harcourt

Go On

Grade 3

Read "An Invitation." Then answer
Numbers 7 through 12.

An Invitation

Dear Mrs. Connolly,

    I am writing to ask you to come to the Winter Concert at Dove Springs Elementary School this weekend. My choir will sing in the concert, and some children will play songs on xylophones and cymbals.

    You should come because the music will be wonderful. The choir and musicians have been practicing for six weeks. Also, all the performers will wear traditional costumes from other countries. We will look very interesting!

    The concert is Saturday at 7 P.M. I hope you can come.

             Your neighbor,
             Julia

7 What will happen at Julia's school on Saturday?

  F a softball game

  G an end-of-the-year party

  H a music concert

  I a fire drill

Go On

Lesson 16

8 Who is Mrs. Connolly?

Ⓐ a teacher

Ⓑ a neighbor

Ⓒ a principal

Ⓓ the mother of Julia's friend

9 Mrs. Connolly should come to the school just before

Ⓕ noon.　　　　Ⓗ five o'clock.

Ⓖ three o'clock.　Ⓘ seven o'clock.

10 The purpose of the second paragraph is to

Ⓐ ask Mrs. Connolly a question.

Ⓑ complain about rehearsals.

Ⓒ persuade Mrs. Connolly to come.

Ⓓ explain Julia's absence from school.

11 A xylophone is probably a kind of

Ⓕ notebook.　　Ⓗ instrument.

Ⓖ stage light.　Ⓘ song.

12 Based on the letter, which of the following statements is true?

Ⓐ Julia needs a costume for the concert.

Ⓑ The concert is at 1 P.M.

Ⓒ The choir has been practicing for a few days.

Ⓓ Some children will play guitars.

STOP

Read the article "Explore with Microscopes."
Then answer Numbers 1 through 8.

Explore with Microscopes

Some people like to explore big places in the world, such as the rain forest or the bottom of the ocean. Other people like to find out about small things. What will you see if you cut open a green pea? How can you find out what a cat hair really looks like? The best way to find out about small things is to use a microscope. Microscopes make tiny things look big.

Most microscopes have two lenses. Lenses are like mirrors that <u>magnify</u> tiny things and make them look bigger. To use a microscope, place what you want to look at on the flat surface. The flat surface is called the "stage."

Lighting is important. The right lighting helps you see into the tiny world on your stage. If the object you are looking at is see-through, put a light under the stage. This way the light will shine up through the object. If the object is not see-through, put the light above the stage. Then the light will shine down on the object.

Place your eye against the eyepiece, and look through the microscope. Use the big knob on the side of the tube to fix the first focus. This moves the stage closer to the eyepiece or farther away. Stop when the object looks almost clear. Then twist the fine focus while you <u>peer</u> through the eyepiece again. Keep fixing the fine focus until the object looks perfectly clear. Now you can really explore this new, little world.

Go On

Name _____

Now answer Numbers 1 through 8. Base your answers on the article "Exploring with Microscopes."

1 What would be a good title for the article?

Ⓐ "How to Use a Microscope"

Ⓑ "Using Lights"

Ⓒ "Eating Green Peas"

Ⓓ "Exploring Large Things"

2 What should you do after you put an object on the stage?

Ⓕ Adjust the focus.

Ⓖ Make sure the object is lit.

Ⓗ Look at the object.

Ⓘ Step away from the eyepiece.

3 Another word or phrase for *magnify* would be

Ⓐ make tiny.

Ⓑ make bigger.

Ⓒ mirror.

Ⓓ light.

4 Where is the first focus knob located?

Ⓕ around the lens

Ⓖ near the eyepiece

Ⓗ below the stage

Ⓘ on the side of the tube

Go On

© Harcourt

5 What does the word *peer* mean in this article?

  Ⓐ look

  Ⓑ knob

  Ⓒ magnify

  Ⓓ platform

6 How many lenses do most microscopes have?

  Ⓕ none

  Ⓖ three

  Ⓗ two

  Ⓘ one

7 What happens when you turn the focus knob? Use facts from the selection to support your answer.

READ
THINK
EXPLAIN

_____

_____

_____

_____

_____

_____

_____

_____

© Harcourt

Go On

Lesson 17

8 READ THINK EXPLAIN

Tell which one of the following people would most likely use a microscope on the job: a *fisherman*, a *doctor*, a *journalist*. Explain your answer.

_____

_____

_____

_____

_____

_____

_____

_____

_____

_____

_____

STOP

Grade 3

Read the story "Karina's Clever Idea."
Then answer Numbers 1 through 5.

Karina's Clever Idea

"I can't wait to get there!" thought Karina as she brushed her teeth. That morning she and her parents would drive to Port Aransas, Texas, to see Karina's aunt and uncle. Once they arrived, Karina would put on her bathing suit. Then she and her aunt would watch seagulls together.

Karina finished dressing and packed her soap and shampoo in her suitcase. "But where can I pack my toothbrush?" she wondered. "I don't want my clothes to get wet!"

Karina thought for a second. Then she ran downstairs. When she came back, she had a plastic bag and a twist tie. She put the toothbrush in the bag and closed the bag with a twist tie.

"Now I'm ready," she said. "Port Aransas, here I come!"

1 What problem does Karina have?

Ⓐ She wants to go to Port Aransas.

Ⓑ She's going to the beach and can't find her bathing suit.

Ⓒ She misses her aunt and uncle.

Ⓓ Her toothbrush is wet, and she needs to pack it.

Go On

2 How does Karina solve her problem?

   (F) She goes to Port Aransas with her sister.

   (G) She puts her toothbrush in a plastic bag.

   (H) She calls her grandparents.

   (I) She borrows a swimsuit from her sister.

3 What is the second thing Karina will do when she gets to Port Aransas?

   (A) put on her swimsuit

   (B) watch seagulls

   (C) brush her teeth

   (D) pack her bag

4 Where is Karina?

   (F) at home   (H) at the mall

   (G) at the beach   (I) at school

---

5 What is Karina like? What does she enjoy doing? Use details from the story to support your answers.

READ
THINK
EXPLAIN

_____

_____

_____

_____

_____

Go On

Grade 3

Read the article "Packing Tips." Then answer Numbers 6 through 11.

Packing Tips

Everyone loves to travel, but packing for a trip can be <u>nerve-wracking</u>. Here are some tips to help you pack your bags without getting stressed out!

- Begin several days before your trip. On a piece of paper, write down the kinds of things you need to pack, like *socks* and *shampoo*.

- Decide how many of each item you will need.

- On the night before your trip, lay out all the items on your bed. Pack everything except items you will need in the morning.

- Just before you leave, put the final items in your bag. Pack your list so that you can keep track of your things during your trip.

Bon Voyage!

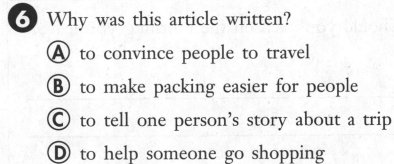

6 Why was this article written?

  A to convince people to travel

  B to make packing easier for people

  C to tell one person's story about a trip

  D to help someone go shopping

7 In this article, *nerve-wracking* probably means

  F stressful.   **H** entertaining.

  G fun.   **I** heavy.

Go On

8 When should people begin to list what they need to bring on a trip?

(A) a few weeks before they leave

(B) a few days before they leave

(C) the night before they leave

(D) an hour before they leave

9 According to the article, what should you do on the night before your trip?

(F) talk with friends

(G) pack everything except what you need in the morning

(H) get a good night's sleep

(I) iron everything you want to pack in your suitcase

10 Right before you leave, pack your

(A) socks.   (C) shoes.

(B) T-shirts.   (D) list.

---

11 What kinds of things should you pack on the morning you leave? Explain.

READ
THINK
EXPLAIN

_____

_____

_____

_____

_____

STOP

Grade 3

Read the story "Lost and Found." Then answer Numbers 1 through 8.

Lost and Found

"Why do we have to go to the police station?" Jimmy asked. He was a little nervous. Only police officers and bad guys went to the police station. Jimmy knew that from TV.

"Remember the backpack we found in the park?" his dad asked. "Well, we need to tell the police about it."

"Why can't we keep it?" Jimmy said. "It's just a backpack." He wondered why they were going to all this trouble for one backpack. There were so many other things they could do today.

"What if you lost your backpack?" Dad said. "You would want someone to turn it in, right?" Jimmy thought about that while his dad parked the car in back of the police station.

Jimmy held his dad's hand as they went into the police station. A woman was sitting at a desk. She wore a police uniform, but she didn't look scary. As a matter of fact, she looked very pleasant.

"How can I help you?" she asked Jimmy's dad. She listened as Jimmy's dad told her about the backpack.

Meanwhile, Jimmy looked around the station. There were no bad guys in handcuffs! This was just a clean, quiet room with booklets and flyers. It didn't seem scary at all.

Jimmy looked at the booklets. There were some that told about neighborhood watch workshops or tips on keeping your house safe. Some had information about when to call 911 for help. There was even a flyer about a summer program for the children in town.

Go On

© Harcourt

"Come on, Jimmy," his dad called, holding the door. "We're all done. The police will take it from here."

Jimmy took one of the flyers. Maybe he'd try a program this summer, he thought. The activities sounded fun and interesting. Besides, it would be fun to come back to the police station.

Now answer Numbers 1 through 8. Base your answers on the story "Lost and Found."

1 What was the first thing Jimmy saw inside the police station?

Ⓐ a waiting room

Ⓑ a woman sitting at a desk

Ⓒ booklets and flyers

Ⓓ a backpack

2 What words best describe the police station?

Ⓕ loud and scary

Ⓖ noisy and busy

Ⓗ quiet and comfortable

Ⓘ dirty and crowded

3 Why were Jimmy and his dad going to the police station?

Ⓐ Jimmy wanted to join a program for neighborhood children.

Ⓑ Jimmy was in trouble.

Ⓒ They found a backpack in the park.

Ⓓ They wanted to learn how to keep their house safe.

Go On

© Harcourt

4 What did Jimmy NOT see in the police station?

    F bad guys

    G a woman behind a desk

    H booklets

    I a police uniform

5 Which answer best summarizes the story?

    A Jimmy says he won't go back to the police station.

    B Jimmy sees that the police station is not a scary or bad place.

    C Jimmy's dad decides to keep the backpack.

    D Jimmy's dad talks to a police officer.

6

READ
THINK
EXPLAIN

Do you think Jimmy was surprised when he walked into the police station? Explain your answer.

_____

_____

_____

_____

_____

_____

_____

_____

© Harcourt

Go On

7 Describe how Jimmy felt about going to the police station. Use information from the story to support your answer.

READ
THINK
EXPLAIN

_____

_____

_____

_____

_____

_____

8 Do you think Jimmy will try one of the summer programs that he read about at the police station? Give reasons for your answer.

READ
THINK
EXPLAIN

_____

_____

_____

_____

_____

_____

STOP

Grade 3

Read the article "Main Street." Then answer Numbers 1 through 6.

Main Street

Many towns in the United States have a main street. The street might be called Main Street, First Avenue, or Center Street. No matter what name the street has, it's probably where the town first began.

Why did towns start with Main Street as the center? Perhaps the street was near the railroad tracks. Maybe it was near the river.

Over the years the street may have changed. One store was built, and others soon followed. Then, as people moved to the area, houses were built. A church and a school followed. Then a barbershop, a restaurant, and even a bank might have been added to Main Street.

The first Main Street was different from Main Street today. The dirt street was busy with horse-drawn wagons and trolley cars. Gas lamps lit the fronts of buildings.

Then the town really began to grow. Many businesses moved into the area. More houses were built, and streets were added.

Time passed and the town continued to change. Cars and trucks replaced horses and carriages. Stores and shopping centers grew on the edges of town.

Then the mall was born. People began to shop at the mall rather than in the stores on Main Street.

What happened to Main Street? Because people were not shopping there, many stores went out of business. New businesses did not replace the old ones. Main Street was becoming empty.

In some towns, though, Main Street is coming back.

Go On

Name _____

Now answer Numbers 1 through 6. Base your answers on the article "Main Street."

1 What is this article mostly about?

Ⓐ the kinds of shops on Main Street

Ⓑ how Main Street changed over time

Ⓒ how people are trying to bring Main Street back

Ⓓ why some towns do not have a Main Street

2 Main Street usually formed the center of town because it was near

Ⓕ city hall or the church.

Ⓖ railroad tracks or a river.

Ⓗ a forest or a meadow.

Ⓘ the town jail or a schoolhouse.

3 Name two ways in which Main Street looked different when the town was founded.

_____

_____

_____

_____

_____

_____

_____

Go On

4 Why was this article written?

Ⓐ to convince people to live on Main Street

Ⓑ to tell an entertaining story about Main Street

Ⓒ to tell people about how Main Street changed over time

Ⓓ to encourage people to visit Main Street in their towns

5 According to the article, the town *really* began to grow because

Ⓕ malls were no longer interesting.

Ⓖ many houses and streets were built and added.

Ⓗ most businesses left the area.

Ⓘ it was built near the railroad tracks.

6 Why did Main Street become empty when malls opened? Use details from the selection in your answer.

READ
THINK
EXPLAIN

_____

_____

_____

_____

_____

_____

_____

STOP

Lesson 20

FCAT Writing

From time to time, everyone sees something new or different. You might see something new in a place you are visiting, or you might see new things in your home or classroom. Think of a time when you saw something new or different. Now describe what you saw and how it made you feel.

Plan and write your essay on separate sheets of paper.

This checklist shows you what your writing must have to receive your best score.

Checklist

I will earn my best score if:

⇨ My essay has a beginning, a middle, and an end.

⇨ My essay tells what I saw and how it made me feel.

⇨ I use details to show what I saw and how I felt about it.

⇨ I use colorful words that describe what I saw clearly, and I do not use the same words over and over.

⇨ Each sentence and proper name begins with a capital letter.

⇨ Each sentence ends with a period, an exclamation point, or a question mark.

© Harcourt

Read the story "William's Last Ride." Then answer Numbers 1 through 5.

William's Last Ride

"Giddyup, Bess!" William said to his horse as he climbed into the saddle. Bess took off at a gallop toward the setting sun.

William was a rider for the Pony Express, which carried mail from St. Louis, Missouri, to California. Whenever he carried mail, William rode very fast all day and all night. When he and his horse made it to the next station, a new rider and horse took the mail and headed farther west.

Now William was taking his last ride. The telegraph had just been invented, and people didn't need pony riders to carry mail or news anymore.

William wasn't too worried about what he would do now. He knew several farmers who would like to hire him. But as he watched the sun drop before him and heard Bess whinny, he knew he would miss riding for the Pony Express.

1 When does the story probably take place?

Ⓐ before cars were invented

Ⓑ after airplanes were invented

Ⓒ before saddles were invented

Ⓓ after phones were invented

Go On

© Harcourt

2 What time of day does William probably start his ride?

   Ⓕ early morning

   Ⓖ noon

   Ⓗ early afternoon

   Ⓘ early evening

3 How does the invention of the telegraph change William's life?

   Ⓐ He will go to school.

   Ⓑ He will move out west.

   Ⓒ He will lose his job.

   Ⓓ He will make money from his invention.

4 How does William probably feel?

   Ⓕ sad

   Ⓖ lonely

   Ⓗ impatient

   Ⓘ sick

5 After his last ride, where will William probably work?

   Ⓐ in a telegraph office

   Ⓑ on a talk show

   Ⓒ on a farm

   Ⓓ in a grocery store

Go On

Read the story "Mystery Mail." Then answer Numbers 6 through 11.

Mystery Mail

Erik opened the mailbox and pulled out several letters.

"I wonder if there's anything for me," he thought.

As he flipped through the letters, he noticed one letter that was different from the rest. The paper was very thin, and the return address was a place in Germany.

Erik went inside. He found his mother in the study. "Mom, who do we know in Germany?" he asked. He handed her the letter.

"Oh, this is from your Uncle Fritz!" she said. "You haven't met him yet. He lives in Berlin."

"Will I ever get to meet him?" Erik asked.

"It looks as though you'll meet him soon," Mom said, smiling. "He's coming to the United States this summer!"

6 At the beginning of the story, Erik

   F goes to school for a baseball game.

   G goes to the post office to get stamps.

   H gets the mail.

   I gets the flu.

7 How is one envelope different from the others?

   A It is brown.   **C** It is thin.

   B It is muddy.   **D** It is typed.

© Harcourt

Go On

8 Which of these events happened first?

  Ⓕ Erik hands his mother the letter.

  Ⓖ Erik notices one letter is different from
     the rest.

  Ⓗ Erik went inside, and he found his mother
     in the study.

  Ⓘ Erik meets Uncle Fritz in the summer.

9 Why hasn't Erik met his Uncle Fritz?

  Ⓐ Erik does not want to travel to Germany.

  Ⓑ Uncle Fritz is afraid of flying.

  Ⓒ Uncle Fritz lives in another country.

  Ⓓ Uncle Fritz does not want to meet Erik.

10 What new thing will Erik probably do later?

  Ⓕ send a letter to a friend

  Ⓖ play soccer with his family

  Ⓗ meet his Uncle Fritz

  Ⓘ go to Germany

---

11 How is the setting of "Mystery Mail" different from the setting of
"William's Last Ride"?

READ
THINK
EXPLAIN

_____

_____

_____

_____

_____

© Harcourt

STOP

Grade 3

**Read the article "Building Materials."
Then answer Numbers 1 through 7.**

Building Materials

In most places where there are people, there are buildings. A building is a structure with four walls and a roof, and it can be made of many different materials. Some buildings are made from materials found nearby. For example, if there are only palm leaves, the buildings will be made of palm leaves. Most often, however, builders use wood, stone, or brick.

No matter what other materials are used, most buildings have some wood in them. Because wood is light, it is easy to work with. Over time, builders have learned that some wood is better for use in buildings than others. The wood from oak and elm trees is the best. These woods are called hardwoods. Today, houses with hardwood beams and floors are very popular.

People have built with bricks for more than 6,000 years. Bricks are easy to use, and they can be made in different sizes. Bricklayers often make intricate patterns with bricks. Some builders use bricks for entire houses, but others use them just for chimneys or walkways. Throughout the world you can still see ancient and medieval cities that are <u>enclosed</u> within brick walls. These walled cities tell us that bricks are strong and can last for centuries.

Unlike wood and brick, stone is not often used to build buildings. It is used to decorate them. There are several reasons for this. Stone is hard, heavy, and expensive. Also, not many people know how to work with stone. Today, marble, granite, slate, and sandstone are used to make parts of a building beautiful.

Go On

© Harcourt

What materials are used in the houses in your community? Has an earthquake, a tornado, or a hurricane ever struck your area? What would happen to the buildings if this occurred?

Builders have to think of these things. They ask and answer many questions before they begin a building.

Now answer Numbers 1 through 7. Base your answers on the article "Building Materials."

1 According to the article, it is best to use the wood from oak and elm trees because both types of wood

  A are light.

  B are expensive.

  C come in different sizes.

  D are hard.

2 Why are fewer stone buildings built today?

  F Not many people know how to work with stone.

  G People don't like stone.

  H Stone is cold and ugly.

  I Stone is hard to find.

3 What is the main idea of the article?

  A Most buildings are made from wood, brick, or stone.

  B It is difficult to build a building.

  C Bricklayers are the best builders.

  D Building buildings is a good profession.

Go On

4 What does the word *enclosed* mean in this article?

   F outside

   G inside

   H old

   I aging

5 Which of these is a kind of stone?

   A elm

   B palm

   C oak

   D granite

6 If you were building a house, would you use wood, brick, or stone? Explain your answer.

READ
THINK
EXPLAIN

_____

_____

_____

_____

_____

_____

_____

Go On

7 What fact from this article did you find most interesting or unusual? Tell why.

READ
THINK
EXPLAIN

_____

_____

_____

_____

_____

_____

_____

_____

_____

_____

_____

© Harcourt

STOP

Grade 3

Read the article "Music in the Air—and on the Page!" Then answer Numbers 1 through 6.

Music in the Air— and on the Page!

Everyone loves to listen to music. Did you know that you can read music, too?

Think about times when you have sung songs from a songbook. Above the words to the song, you probably noticed five long lines. These lines are called a staff, and the markings on them are called notes. The notes stand for different <u>pitches</u>, or high and low sounds.

Every note has a name, but you don't need to know the names to read music. Just remember that the note on the bottom line is a low note, and the note on the top line is a high note. The other notes are somewhere in between. Try to make your voice higher or lower as you see the notes climb up or down the scale.

1 Why was this article written?

   Ⓐ to tell about a special songbook

   Ⓑ to convince people to take music lessons

   Ⓒ to teach people how to read music

   Ⓓ to tell what makes voices high or low

2 A staff is made up of

   Ⓕ two lines.   Ⓗ four lines.

   Ⓖ three lines.   Ⓘ five lines.

Go On

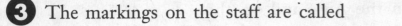

3 The markings on the staff are called

Ⓐ music.

Ⓑ songs.

Ⓒ notes.

Ⓓ spaces.

4 What does the word *pitches* mean in this article?

Ⓕ throws

Ⓖ sounds

Ⓗ lines

Ⓘ scales

5 To read music, it is important to know

Ⓐ the names of different notes.

Ⓑ the words to a song.

Ⓒ where the high and low notes are.

Ⓓ how to breathe deeply.

6 Where does the staff usually appear in a songbook?

Ⓕ below the words of a song

Ⓖ above the words of a song

Ⓗ at the beginning of the book

Ⓘ at the end of the book

Go On

Grade 3

Read the story "Wendy's Recital." Then answer Numbers 7 through 12.

Wendy's Recital

Wendy stood backstage and peeked through a crack in the curtain. The <u>auditorium</u> was almost full. Lots of people had driven through the snowstorm to hear Mrs. Engel's students play the piano.

Suddenly, Wendy heard Mrs. Engel say, "Our first pianist is Wendy Chang!"

"That's me!" she thought, and she hurried onstage. Her heart was pounding. <u>She bowed to the audience. Then she sat in front of the keys</u>. Her hands felt cold and stiff. But when she played the first note, she felt her whole body relax. Then she knew she would do just fine.

7 An *auditorium* is a place where people

(A) watch and listen.   (C) talk.

(B) eat and relax.   (D) exercise.

8 The story takes place in

(F) spring.   (H) fall.

(G) summer.   (I) winter.

9 How does Wendy feel when she steps onto the stage?

(A) relaxed   (C) lonely

(B) nervous   (D) smart

© Harcourt

Go On

10 What sentence from the story supports your answer to question 9?

(F) Her heart was pounding.

(G) She bowed to the audience.

(H) Then she sat in front of the keys.

(I) Then she knew she would do just fine.

11 Look at the underlined sentences in paragraph 3. The sentences tell that Wendy

(A) was finished performing.

(B) was about to begin performing.

(C) was nervous about performing.

(D) was excited about performing.

12 How does Wendy change when she begins to play?

READ
THINK
EXPLAIN

_____

_____

_____

_____

_____

_____

_____

_____

STOP

Grade 3

Name _____

Read the story "Emil Plays the Piano."
Then answer Numbers 1 through 9.

Emil Plays the Piano

Every day on the way to the bus stop, Emil would pass the music store. Through the window he could see the big black piano. It looked so pretty that Emil wanted to touch it. There was never any time as he and his mother hurried to catch the bus.

Then one day the bus came early. Even though they ran, Emil and his mother couldn't catch it. They were left huffing and puffing on the sidewalk.

"Now what are we going to do?" his mother asked. "There isn't another bus for half an hour, and it's hot out here."

"Let's go into the music store," Emil said.

"Why would you want to go in there?" his mother asked, but she let Emil guide her into the store.

"Emil! Don't touch anything!" his mother said, just as he was about to touch the piano keys. Emil sighed.

Then a man came from behind the counter. "It's fine," he told Emil's mother. "The piano is there so people can play it."

He helped Emil onto the piano bench. "See?" the man said, playing a few notes. "You press down on one key, and it makes a tune. You press down on three keys, and you get a chord."

Emil nodded. He put his fingers on the same keys the man had pressed. He played one note and then the chord, which pleased Emil. It was the perfect way to end the tune.

Go On

"That was good," the man said. "Do you play music?"

"No," Emil said.

"They have classes at his school," his mother said. "We never thought of having Emil take lessons. Maybe we should, though."

The man nodded. "That's a very good way to start," he said.

Now answer Numbers 1 through 9. Base your answers on the story "Emil Plays the Piano."

 1 What happened right before Emil and his mother went into the music store?

   Ⓐ They bought donuts.

   Ⓑ They missed the bus.

   Ⓒ They sang a song.

   Ⓓ They got a flat tire.

2 On what kind of day did this story take place?

   Ⓕ a hot day

   Ⓖ a rainy day

   Ⓗ a cold day

   Ⓘ a snowy day

3 What do you think Emil's mother will do next?

   Ⓐ She will sign Emil up for music lessons.

   Ⓑ She will forget about the visit to the store.

   Ⓒ She will scold Emil for touching the piano.

   Ⓓ She will get a new bus schedule.

Go On

4 According to this story, what does the word
guide mean?

(F) read

(G) sing

(H) lead

(I) a book with directions

5 Which sentence best describes what happened
in this story?

(A) Emil decided he didn't like music.

(B) Emil showed that he could learn to play
the piano.

(C) Emil's mother decided to buy a piano.

(D) Emil discovered that he loved the saxophone.

6 Why did Emil and his mother go into the music store?

READ
THINK
EXPLAIN

_____

_____

_____

_____

_____

_____

_____

Go On

7 How do you think Emil felt at the end of the story?

Ⓕ bored and restless

Ⓖ nervous and confused

Ⓗ pleased and proud

Ⓘ embarrassed and regretful

8

READ
THINK
EXPLAIN

The man from the music store tells how to make a tune and how to make a chord. In your own words, tell how to make each sound.

_____

_____

_____

_____

_____

9

READ
THINK
EXPLAIN

Based on what the author has told you about Emil, do you think that he will learn to play the piano some day? Give reasons for your answer.

_____

_____

_____

_____

_____

STOP

Grade 3

Read the article "Bees at Work." Then answer Numbers 1 through 8.

Bees at Work

In every hive there are three kinds of bees: the queen, the drones, and the workers. The queen and the drones work to lay eggs, so that new bees will be born. The workers run the hive, keeping it healthy and <u>comfortable</u>. The workers also do things to make the hive a nice place to live, such as finding food for the other bees.

Worker bees like to build beehives in hidden places, such as inside hollow logs. Using wax, they make groups of cells known as *combs*. The queen lays one egg inside each cell.

It takes about fifteen days for each bee to hatch. These new bees stay in the nest. Their job is to help clean out used cells and to feed the next set of baby bees. Then the new worker bees learn to make wax. They use the wax to repair or make new cells.

As a worker bee gets older, its job changes. Its next job might be to guard the opening to the hive. Guarding is an important job, and one that is filled with danger. A bee can be killed while guarding the hive.

Finally, older worker bees get to fly out of the hive. They look in flowers for nectar and pollen, which the bees use for food.

1 What does *comfortable* mean, as used in this article?

    A pleasant   **C** awful

    B busy   **D** alive

Go On

© Harcourt

1. What is the main job of the drone?

   (F) to gather food for the hive

   (G) to guard the entrance of the hive

   (H) to help the queen lay new eggs

   (I) to take care of the baby bees

3 What do the bees use to make and repair cells in the hive?

   (A) nectar   (C) combs

   (B) pollen   (D) wax

4. What job do the worker bees have after guarding the entrance of the hive?

   (F) They build and repair cells.

   (G) They help gather food.

   (H) They help the queen lay new eggs.

   (I) They take care of the baby bees.

---

5 Describe the beehive made by the bees. Use information from the article in your answer.

READ
THINK
EXPLAIN

_____

_____

_____

_____

_____

_____

_____

© Harcourt

Go On

6 What is the first job worker bees have after they are born?

Ⓐ They clean cells.

Ⓑ They help the queen lay eggs.

Ⓒ They find food for the hive.

Ⓓ They make wax.

7 Why do you think the author wrote this article?

Ⓕ to warn people about bees

Ⓖ to tell an amusing story about bees

Ⓗ to teach people about bees

Ⓘ to convince people that bees are important to humans

8 Why is the worker bee so important to the hive?

READ
THINK
EXPLAIN

_____

_____

_____

_____

_____

_____

_____

STOP

Lesson 25

FCAT Writing

If you are like most people, you probably have a favorite sport. How is it played? Does it have special rules, and do people need any special equipment to play it? Write a composition to describe your favorite sport to someone who has never played it or seen it.

Plan and write your composition on separate sheets of paper.

The checklist below shows what your story must have to receive the best score.

Checklist

I will earn my best score if:

⇨ My composition has a beginning, a middle, and an end.

⇨ My composition tells what my favorite sport is and how it is played.

⇨ I use details to make my favorite sport clear to someone who has never seen it or played it.

⇨ I use words that make my meaning clear, and I do not use the same words over and over.

⇨ Each sentence and proper name begins with a capital letter.

⇨ Each sentence ends with a period, an exclamation point, or a question mark.

© Harcourt

**Read the story "Firefly Lamps."
Then answer Numbers 1 through 6.**

Firefly Lamps

Jason sat on his back porch on a warm evening.
He watched the fireflies blink on and off in
the yard.

"I wish I could keep a firefly for a pet," he
thought. But Jason knew that fireflies can not <u>survive</u>
long if they are kept as pets.

Just then Jason had an idea. He went to the kitchen
and found six large glass jars with lids. He asked his
dad to cut holes in the lids for him. Then Jason went
back outside and caught a firefly for each jar.

Jason placed the jars along the edge of the porch.
He would free the fireflies very soon, but for a few
minutes, he wanted to enjoy his firefly lamps.

1 In this story, *survive* probably means the same as

   (A) sing.

   (B) blink.

   (C) live.

   (D) eat.

2 Why does Jason have his dad cut holes in the lids?

   (F) to make the jars prettier

   (G) so he can put coins through the holes

   (H) so he can sip water from the jars

   (I) so the fireflies can breathe

Go On

3 What is the setting of the story?

Ⓐ a backyard in early summer

Ⓑ a backyard in late fall

Ⓒ a campsite in early summer

Ⓓ a campsite in late fall

4 What does Jason wish he could do?

Ⓕ sleep on the porch

Ⓖ keep a firefly as a pet

Ⓗ fly like a firefly

Ⓘ buy lanterns

5 What does he decide to do instead?

Ⓐ go camping

Ⓑ watch television

Ⓒ catch fireflies and let them go

Ⓓ have a picnic on the porch

6 What do you know about Jason from the way he treats the fireflies? Use details from the story to support your answer.

READ
THINK
EXPLAIN

_____

_____

_____

_____

_____

_____

Go On

Grade 3

© Harcourt

Read "A Summer Letter." Then answer Numbers 7 through 12.

A Summer Letter

Dear Clarissa,

   How is your summer? Mine is great so far. Last week my parents and I camped on the beach. We cooked dinner on a campfire, and then we sat around and sang songs. When the campfire went out, we looked up and counted as many stars as we could see.

   I think the beach is a hard place to camp. The wind off the water can be strong. Sometimes it blew sand into my eyes and hair. The beach is also very pretty. There are interesting birds and shells. I would like to camp there again. Maybe you can come next time!

                    Your friend,
                    Anita

7 Anita has been to

(F) the mountains.　(H) the beach.

(G) the woods.　(I) her grandmother's house.

8 From the letter, Clarissa probably thinks that Anita is

(A) not enjoying her summer.

(B) anxious to go home.

(C) excited about her camping trip.

(D) annoyed by the strong wind.

Go On

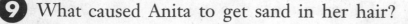

9 What caused Anita to get sand in her hair?

F her brother Andrew

G a bird

H a strong wind

I lying on the beach

10 According to the letter, it is hard to camp on the beach because

A it is pretty.

B there are a lot of stars.

C there are interesting birds.

D the wind is strong.

11 Why did Anita write this letter?

F She is lonely. She wants her friend to come to the beach.

G She is afraid no one knows where she is.

H She wants to tell her friend what fun things she has been doing.

I She wants to get a job as a lifeguard.

12 What do you think Anita likes about the beach? Use details from the letter to support your answer.

READ
THINK
EXPLAIN

_____

_____

_____

_____

_____

© Harcourt

STOP

Grade 3

Name _____

**Read the poem "My Best Friend."
Then answer Numbers 1 through 6.**

My Best Friend

Woof! Woof!

Rover meets me at the door.

Woof! Woof!

He knocks me to the floor!

"Sit! Stay!" I yell

and try to stand.

But Rover is glad to see me

so he knocks me down again!

1 This passage must be from a poem because

Ⓐ it has short lines.

Ⓑ it is about a dog.

Ⓒ it has a title.

Ⓓ it has a speaker.

2 What kind of sound is *woof*?

Ⓕ a meow

Ⓖ a chirp

Ⓗ a roar

Ⓘ a bark

Go On

© Harcourt

3 Rover is probably

   Ⓐ obedient.

   Ⓑ quiet.

   Ⓒ excited.

   Ⓓ unhappy.

4 The speaker probably

   Ⓕ dislikes animals.

   Ⓖ enjoys animals.

   Ⓗ wants to give Rover away.

   Ⓘ wishes Rover was more active.

5 In the poem, line 1 and line 3

   Ⓐ rhyme.

   Ⓑ are the same.

   Ⓒ tell the speaker's thoughts.

   Ⓓ tell the speaker's words.

6 Why did the speaker write this poem?

   Ⓕ to share a funny story about his dog

   Ⓖ to make his dog happy

   Ⓗ to give his classmates information about dogs

   Ⓘ to convince people to adopt dogs

Go On

Grade 3

Read the story "Along for the Ride."
Then answer Numbers 7 through 12.

Along for the Ride

Sylvia had a new baby brother. His name was
Henry. Every day after school, Sylvia and her
mother took Henry for a stroller ride. The stroller
was big and had a basket attached to its <u>underside</u>.

One afternoon, Mom carried Henry's diaper bag
during their walk. It was very heavy. Sylvia could
see that Mom was getting tired.

"Mom, why don't I put the bag in the basket under
the stroller?"

"That's a good idea!" said Mom. Sylvia took the
bag from Mom. She leaned down to put the bag in
the basket. Just then, Peaches, the family cat, jumped
out of the basket and stood by Sylvia's feet.

Sylvia laughed. "Mom, it looks like Peaches likes
stroller rides, too!"

7 Every afternoon Sylvia and her mother

Ⓐ go outside.

Ⓑ take the baby for a stroller ride.

Ⓒ play with the cat.

Ⓓ have a snack after school.

8 What problem does Mom have with the
diaper bag?

Ⓕ It has a hole.   Ⓗ It is too heavy.

Ⓖ It is ugly.   Ⓘ It has a broken strap.

Go On

9 How does Sylvia solve Mom's problem?

Ⓐ She carries the bag.

Ⓑ She returns the bag to the store.

Ⓒ She sews a patch on the bag.

Ⓓ She offers to put the bag in the stroller basket.

10 Where is the *underside* of the stroller?

Ⓕ on top of the seat

Ⓖ on the left side

Ⓗ on the right side

Ⓘ beneath the seat

---

11 What happens at the end of the story?

READ
THINK
EXPLAIN

_____

_____

_____

_____

_____

---

12 How does Sylvia probably feel at the end of the story?
Give details from the story to support your answer.

READ
THINK
EXPLAIN

_____

_____

_____

_____

_____

© Harcourt

STOP

Grade 3

Name _____

Read the story "How We Got the Indian Paintbrush Flower." Then complete Numbers 1 through 9.

How We Got the Indian Paintbrush Flower

A long time ago, a small boy lived on the plains. He loved to work with his hands, making pretty things.

One day, the boy fell asleep on a hilltop and had a dream. He dreamed he was given tools for painting. Also in his dream, a wise person told him that one day he would paint a wonderful picture of the evening sky.

When the boy woke up, he started to paint. His pictures made people happy, but one thing always bothered him. He could never find the right colors to paint the sunset.

One evening the boy climbed back up the hill. At the top, he found paintbrushes on the ground. The brushes were filled with all the colors he needed. He picked up the brushes and painted the beautiful sunset.

The boy left his brushes on the hillside. The next morning, he discovered that his paintbrushes had grown into flowers. That is how we got the Indian paintbrush flowers that <u>brighten</u> the hillsides of the West every spring.

Go On

© Harcourt

Now answer Numbers 1 through 9. Base your answers on the story "How We Got the Indian Paintbrush Flower."

1 The boy lives on

Ⓐ a mountain.　　Ⓒ a hilltop.

Ⓑ the plains.　　Ⓓ a river.

2 The story is an example of

Ⓕ a play.　　Ⓗ a myth.

Ⓖ a poem.　　Ⓘ a news article.

3 What does the boy like to do?

Ⓐ ride on ponies

Ⓑ make things with his hands

Ⓒ work in the garden

Ⓓ sleep all day

4 What happens the first time the boy climbs to the top of the hill?

Ⓕ He picks a flower.

Ⓖ He falls asleep.

Ⓗ He speaks to a wise man.

Ⓘ He rolls down the side of the hill.

5 What problem does the boy have?

Ⓐ He can't ride a horse.

Ⓑ He does not have paper for painting.

Ⓒ He can't find the right colors of paint.

Ⓓ He does not want to be a painter.

Go On

© Harcourt

6 How is the boy's problem solved?

   Ⓕ Someone teaches him to ride a horse.

   Ⓖ He becomes a wise man.

   Ⓗ His mother buys paper for him.

   Ⓘ He finds brushes filled with paint.

7 What does the word *brighten* mean in the story?

   Ⓐ makes bright

   Ⓑ makes young

   Ⓒ says bright

   Ⓓ makes dark

8 What helped you know that flowers would appear at the end of the story?

READ
THINK
EXPLAIN

_____

_____

_____

_____

_____

_____

_____

Go On

Lesson 28

9 How does the boy solve his problem? Use details from the story.

READ
THINK
EXPLAIN

_____

_____

_____

_____

_____

_____

_____

_____

_____

_____

_____

_____

STOP

Grade 3

Read the story "Mrs. Small's Gift." Then answer Numbers 1 through 6.

Mrs. Small's Gift

Jada and Catherine really liked their teacher, Mrs. Small. Mrs. Small read stories better than anyone else.

When Mrs. Small said she would not be teaching next year, Jada and Catherine knew that they would miss her.

"Let's get a present for her before she leaves," said Catherine.

Jada and Catherine searched all over the mall. They could not find anything they liked.

"Let's look in just one more store," said Catherine.

They walked into the card store. On a tiny shelf there was a statue of a woman reading to a group of children.

"This is perfect!" said Jada. "When Mrs. Small looks at this statue, she will think of us!"

1 What does Mrs. Small tell her class?

  Ⓐ She has a cold.

  Ⓑ She wants to start their lesson.

  Ⓒ She will not teach at their school the next year.

  Ⓓ They have a homework assignment this weekend.

2 What do Jada and Catherine want to do for Mrs. Small?

  Ⓕ clean her erasers

  Ⓖ buy her a present

  Ⓗ put books in her reading corner

  Ⓘ feed the class's goldfish

Go On

3 What problem do Jada and Catherine have?

Ⓐ They do not have money.

Ⓑ They do not know what Mrs. Small likes.

Ⓒ They are not able to get to the mall.

Ⓓ They cannot find a gift they like for Mrs. Small.

4 How are Jada and Catherine alike?

Ⓕ They both like basketball.

Ⓖ They both like Mrs. Small.

Ⓗ They both eat oatmeal for breakfast.

Ⓘ They like the same books.

5 The theme of this story is

Ⓐ be nice to your favorite teacher.

Ⓑ don't give up hope.

Ⓒ a penny saved is a penny earned.

Ⓓ read a story every day.

6 How is the statue a symbol? Use details from the story to support your answer.

READ
THINK
EXPLAIN

_____

_____

_____

_____

_____

_____

© Harcourt

Go On

Read the "Bake Sale" flyer. Then answer Numbers 7 through 12.

Bake Sale!

Come to the

BAKE SALE!

When: Saturday, October 28;

12 P.M.–1 P.M.

Where: the cafeteria

Sponsored by: the Student Council

Every penny you give will help us raise money to buy new books for the school library. Lots of our library books are falling apart! Others have been lost. We need to replace old books and missing books. We need to buy some newer books, too.

So drop by school on Saturday and buy a goody! Or buy two goodies and share one with a friend! They're delicious! And it's for a good cause.

7 The bake sale will take place on

   F Wednesday.

   G Thursday.

   H Friday.

   I Saturday.

8 Who is sponsoring the bake sale?

   A the Student Council

   B the Girl Scouts

   C the third-grade class

   D the school chorus

Go On

9 Why is the Student Council holding the bake sale?

    Ⓕ The gym needs new mats.

    Ⓖ The music teacher needs new instruments.

    Ⓗ The library needs new books.

    Ⓘ The art teacher needs new paints.

10 Where will the bake sale take place?

    Ⓐ library

    Ⓑ gym

    Ⓒ cafeteria

    Ⓓ school parking lot

11 What is the purpose of this flyer?

    Ⓕ to tell people about the cafeteria

    Ⓖ to let people know about a party

    Ⓗ to get people to come to the bake sale

    Ⓘ to convince people to support the Student Council

12

READ
THINK
EXPLAIN

How is the Student Council similar to and different from Jada and Catherine? Use details from the story and the flyer in your answer.

_____

_____

_____

_____

_____

_____

STOP

Grade 3

Read the story "The Early-Rising Machine."
Then answer Numbers 1 through 10.

An Early-Rising Machine

John Muir liked to invent things. He would wake up very early in the morning. He would go down to the cellar of his home. That is where he built all kinds of things.

Many of his inventions were clocks. He made one clock that had four sides. He made another that did not have the numbers in a circle. He even made a timer to <u>attach</u> to a bed. He called this invention an early-rising machine.

John decided to take his inventions to the State Fair.

At the fair, John saw two young boys. He asked them to help him show how the early-rising machine worked.

The boys pretended to be sleeping in the bed. While John was speaking, the timer kept ticking. When the "wake-up time" came, the early-rising machine made the bed tip up at one end. The boys slid out of the other end. Everybody thought it was great fun!

© Harcourt

Go On

Now answer numbers 1 through 10. Base your answers on the story "The Early-Rising Machine."

1 John Muir was an
   Ⓐ actor.   Ⓒ inventor.
   Ⓑ airplane pilot.   Ⓓ ocean explorer.

❷ Where was John Muir's workroom?
   Ⓕ in the attic   Ⓗ in the basement
   Ⓖ in the bedroom   Ⓘ in the garage

❸ What problem did John Muir probably want to solve?
   Ⓐ oversleeping   Ⓒ mismatched socks
   Ⓑ overeating   Ⓓ wrinkles in clothes

4 In the story, what does the word *attach* mean?
   Ⓕ cover   Ⓗ make up
   Ⓖ stick on   Ⓘ lead

❺ The early-rising machine made the bed tip up when
   Ⓐ the State Fair began.
   Ⓑ the cellar door opened.
   Ⓒ the audience laughed.
   Ⓓ wake-up time came.

❻ What happened when John Muir presented his early-rising machine at the State Fair? Include details from the selection.

READ
THINK
EXPLAIN

_____

_____

_____

_____

© Harcourt

Go On
Grade 3

7 This story is mostly about

   F John Muir's sons.

   G the way John Muir's bed tipped up at one end.

   H John Muir's early-rising machine.

   I two boys who helped John Muir.

8 Most of John Muir's inventions were

   A beds.

   B clocks.

   C alarms.

   D timers.

9 Another name for this article might be

   F Tossed Out of Bed.

   G How Alarm Clocks Work.

   H How to Pretend to be Asleep.

   I Working in the Cellar.

---

10 Which of John Muir's inventions do you want? Why?

READ
THINK
EXPLAIN

_____

_____

_____

_____

_____

_____

© Harcourt

STOP

FCAT Writing

Imagine that you have a wonderful talent that lets you do something nobody else can do. What challenges does this special talent bring? How are the challenges met at the end of the story? Write a story about a talent you have or would like to have and the challenges it creates for you.

Plan and write your story on separate sheets of paper.

This checklist shows you what your writing must have to receive your best score.

Checklist

I will earn my best score if:

⇨ My story has a beginning, a middle, and an end.

⇨ My story tells what my talent is and what challenges it creates.

⇨ I use details and examples to describe my talent, show the challenges, and show how I solved them.

⇨ I use interesting words that make my meaning clear.

⇨ My sentences are varied and complete.

⇨ I use commas, quotation marks, periods, question marks, and exclamation points correctly.

© Harcourt

Grade 3